I'm Free, But It'll Cost You

I'm Free, But It'll Cost You

The Single Life

According to

Kim Coles

HYPERION

New York

ISBN 0–7868–6272–6

Designed by Richard Oriolo

To all my boyfriends, past, present, and future.
I love you.
I hate you.
I miss you.
I want my money back.

Choose the statement that fits you.

Thank you, Ma and Daddy, for giving me great genes and
teaching me how to use them.
Thank you for your support, love, and dedication.

♥

Contents

♥

Acknowledgments

♥

I must thank so many folks whose love and support have been invaluable to me and to this book.

Thank you to:

My family for being consistently encouraging.

My friends who willingly answered the surveys with humor and candor.

My "Living Single" family of staff and crew for all the fun and inspiration over the past few years.

My exceptional castmates for their love and for allowing me to be me: T.C. for your thoughtfulness—the man gives flowers on *every* holiday; John—I pray that I'm around to see you when you are an old man; you are going to be too funny; Kim F.F.—the child/star woman/star, wants to grow old gracefully like Lena Horne and she will/star; Latifah for all the dirty little songs we've made up to amuse ourselves and for allowing me to be your court jester; and "my precious Erika" (as my mother calls her), I am free to go shopping again!

My attorney Matt "Can You Say Re-negotiation" Johnson.

My business manager Errol "Save Your Money" Collier.

Pam "Be Safe Out There" Collier.

Brigid Walsh and Johnathan, I love ya'll.

My assistant Lori for reading and laughing at all the drafts from first to last.

Acknowledgments

Charles Randolph-Wright, Aton Edwards, and Moses Edinborough: the three people in my life who in one way or another were instrumental in showing me that I can and should write.

Lawrence Jordan, my agent par excellence, for carefully navigating my way through the sea of publishing.

Laurie Abkemeier, my editor at Hyperion, for telling me when I was rowing in the right direction.

Monique Zeno, your dedication is without measure. It would've taken me 100 years to finish this without you.

And to my manager and dear friend Mr. Sinclair Jones, don't think that I have forgotten this was your idea in the first place. In all honesty, writing a book was not high on my list of things to do. Thank you for convincing me that this was the right time. Thank you for your passion for this project and for making it happen. Words cannot adequately describe my appreciation of your unswerving belief in me. "Let's take this to a whole other level."

Kim's Disclaimer

♥

The opinions expressed in this book are not necessarily those of the publisher, agent, or typist. They're mine, all mine. I call it like I see it. And like you, sometimes I have on my glasses, sometimes I have on my rose-colored glasses, sometimes I have on my dark shades, and sometimes I have blinders on. And occasionally I'm caught looking the wrong damn way! But no matter what, I have been truthful about my observations, speculations, evaluations, and relations (damn, I'm starting to sound like Jesse Jackson), but admittedly I may not always be right. I am not a psychologist or a sociologist or a licensed therapist, however. I am a single woman living in the nineties and that alone makes me somewhat of an expert. Please, I have lived, loved, lost, and even lived to love again.

I like to refer to myself as an armchair cultural anthropologist. I enjoy digging in, checking it out, and watching it all, and then forming what I hope you will agree will be some really groovy and funny hypotheses.

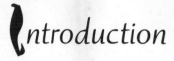Introduction

♥

Okay, so you've read all the other books written by the Ph.D.s of relationships: *Women Are from Pluto, Men Are Goofy*, whatever. You've watched every episode of "Oprah" on how to get, keep, and marry a man by any means necessary. You've gone to church every Sunday and prayed to God to have the reverend ask you over for Sunday brunch, and look at you—your love life is as cold as a polar bear's butt. Not to fret, I come bearing gifts of wisdom for all of my sistahs in search of "Mr. If-the-Ring-Fits-and-It's-a-20-Karat-Marquis-It's Right."

Introduction

Now I know you're thinking right about now: "Why did I buy this book?" Believe me, by the second chapter you will be soooo enlightened and grateful for the knowledge I have espoused that you will rush out and buy a copy of *I'm Free, But It'll Cost You* for a friend. Let me say that again. You will love this book soooo much that you will rush out and buy ten copies for your friends. By the fifth chapter, you will be so entertained by my anecdotes and stories on relationships and men, that if a light bulb hasn't gone off, I suggest you go to your nearest place of worship and fill out an application for the nunnery, because you're just a little too uptight, my sistah.

Are you asked the questions, "Table for one?" or "Is someone using this chair?" on a daily basis? Do people call you on a Friday night to watch *Bebe's Kids* because they know you are available? Instead of saying "His" and "Hers," do your bath towels say, "Mine, Dammit!" Do you have a lifetime subscription to *Chocolate Singles*? Has your father started making a videotape album for the grandchildren he won't be alive to see? If you answered yes to any of the above questions, then you need to read this book.

At the fresh, young, tender age of 21 (yeah, right), I would be a liar if I said I had all the answers to women's dilemmas of dating in the nineties, but I have been on every date from hell imaginable—and unimaginable for that matter. I have survived a marriage and a divorce, and I have learned so much about men that it would just be downright rude to keep it to myself.

I can't guarantee after reading this book that you'll be on your way to the altar, but I *can* guarantee that you'll be cracking up all the way to the bookstore to buy those twenty copies for friends. After all, it's important that we learn to laugh at ourselves, and I don't mean while standing butt-naked in front of a mirror, either. For it was Confucius who said, "He who laughs least, laughs loudest." Or was it, "He who laughs loud, laughs last?" Anyway, if Confucius had been a sistah, her wisdom would have been, "If I ain't married by the time I'm thirty, ain't nobody gonna be laughin'."

Ladies, we have to wise up because even though our *School Daze* have ended, it doesn't have to be all down *Sugar Hill* from here and the *House Party (I, II* and *III)* doesn't have to be over. Black men may be considered a *Menace II Society* but for the *Daughters of the Dust*, these *Boyz N the Hood* who came *Straight Out of Brooklyn* are the *Five Heartbeats* that make life worth living. We must listen to his *Soldier Story* and his *Tales from the Hood* and believe in his *Hoop Dreams*.

Now, do not be fooled by the *Distinguished Gentleman* with *Mo' Money* who dresses real *Fresh,* or buy into *Jason's Lyric* because he's a smooth talker. We're so busy trying to be *The Rich Man's Wife* that we sometimes give the *Shaft* to *The Nutty Professor* who just might be *The Fan* to flame our heart.

And yes, *Jungle Fever* is a *Major Payne*, not to mention a *Low Down Dirty Shame*, but I know our men will *Do the Right Thing* and realize *She's Gotta Have It* just because she's curious. It will be a day of *Glory* when they recognize they are in *Bad Company* and like a *Boomerang* will come back to us doing the *Hollywood Shuffle*. When he recovers from his *Love Jones* with that *Devil in a Blue Dress* it will be *Strictly Business* because he will need to be *Dropped Squad* before he can have some of these *Mo' Better Blues* again.

But ultimately sistahs, we must stop looking like the *Walking Dead* when love *Ricochets* down a wrong alley because we know that *It's a Thin Line Between Love and Hate* and truly *What's Love Got to Do with It* anyway? So let's *Set It Off* with an *Independence Day* of our own. Our *Friday*s should be filled with things to do even if we must *Get on the Bus* in order to go *Solo* to that new club. And girlfriend, don't be shy, go on, *Sparkle*, wear that new dress—*The Color Purple* one you just bought. During this period of self-analysis, we must go under *Deep Cover* and emerge with a *Higher Learning* about ourselves. Only when we stop *Waiting to Exhale* and praying to become *The Preacher's Wife* will there finally be *Poetic Justice* in "Living Single." By the way, have you seen any good movies lately? Whew!

If there is one thing I want you to take from this book, it's that we women must learn to validate ourselves. (It took me the longest time to figure out that Susan L. Taylor of *Essence* wasn't talking about parking validation.) We must learn to decorate our own souls and learn to be happy with self. We must learn to do for self. We do not need a man to make us whole. I repeat: *We do not need a man to validate us.* For Cleopatra ruled Egypt solo, Harriet Tubman discovered the Underground Railroad on her own, and Angela Davis grew that big-ass afro all by her damn self.

Now, before we go any further, I must let you know that this book is not meant to, in any way, offend or disrespect my beautiful Nubian Brothers. Let's get that straight now. It's not your average male-bashing book. It's above average. Just joking! This is not an I-hate-men-and-I'm-taking-out-my-revenge-by-writing-this-book kind of book. I love men. I *really* love black men. Really, any cracks, put-downs, disses, comments that appear to be negative, stereotypical, pernicious, insensitive, unfeeling, unmitigated, derogatory, debasing, hurtful, or opprobrious are only meant in jest, for the most part. (Wow, that thesaurus feature on my computer is all that.)

This book is my attempt to analyze female/male relationships, in a humorous, yet truthful, a whimsical, yet sincere, a facetious, yet candid way. (There I go with the thesaurus again.) So at the end of the book you will have a kinder, gentler appreciation for the opposite sex, yet you'll be ready to get that restraining order at a moment's notice.

Oh yeah, by the way, this book is rated PG and is for everyone over the age of 18. Black women, black men, white women, white men, Hindus, Latinos, Filipinos, Quakers, the Flemish, Jews, Gentiles, Parisians, Istanbuliates, Istanbulionians, Istanbulish . . . huh? Well, you get the idea. I think it will even appeal to barnyard animals. Basically, if you've got $18.95 to spend, the ability to read, and a desire to wade your way through the murky waters of sex, dating, relationships, single-dom, and marriage, then this book may be a lifeboat for you and the thirty friends you bought it for!

I'm Free, But It'll Cost You

♥

Get It Together, or Leave Us Alone

So you're in love again. This man has thrown the sweetest taboo on you. He gives good love. He's got a good job at the post office. He's got a checking account, and then *Bam!*—for your three-month anniversary he gives you a beeper and says he wants to know where you are at all times 'cuz you *his* now! It's always something.

Nowadays, finding your soul mate is harder than trying to take a dump in a public restroom. And if you do meet someone who has potential, it seems to last about as long as those damn ice sculptures you see at banquets because you didn't stop to realize that, other than a high sex drive, the only thing you had in common was both your names began with a B. Sometimes I just wish finding "the one" was as easy as taking a home pregnancy test. You tinkle in a cup, he tinkles in a cup, you mix it together, and dip a stick in it. If there's a plus sign, he's the one. If it's a minus, he ain't the one. And if the stick melts or smoke starts rising from the cup, you should probably consult a doctor.

I had a girlfriend who would determine if her relationships were going to be long-term based solely on her psychic. Every time she would meet a man she would ask her psychic the same question, "Do you see this man in my future?" And every time, the psychic would shake his head no like a surgeon after he reattached an arm, backwards. Now, because the psychic had been on the money in other areas of her life, she would go straight home and fire her new man. It didn't matter if the relationship was going well or not; if the psychic said it wasn't going to last, she wouldn't waste her time. After three years of kicking men to the curb, she finally broke down and asked her psychic when she was finally going to meet her soul mate. The psychic shook his crystal ball and all of a sudden got a gleam in his eye. He predicted that she was going to get a knock on her door at 12 o'clock the following afternoon from a handsome stranger who would be the one. She left in a hurry to prepare for her destiny and sure enough, at noon the next day there was a knock at her door. Too excited and nervous to greet the stranger, she asked her sister to answer the door. Seconds later her sister hollered, "Jana, your psychic is here dressed in a cloak and a fake mustache!" So much for the psychic hotline!

As I always say, men are like a box of chocolates. You don't know what the hell you're going to get. So most of us just close our eyes, take a bite, and hope he ain't the nasty kind with nuts that leaves a bad taste in your mouth. (Get your mind out of the gutter!)

I think before we can truly find a compatible life partner . . . well, maybe not a life partner. Before we can find a significant other . . . well, perhaps that's a little heavy. Before we can find some stranger who we want to fall in love with and sire our children, we must first decide what characteristics we will, and what characteristics we absolutely will *not*, tolerate in a man. For instance, if you know you like the strong, silent type, yet you're in a relationship with a man who has the biggest Friends and Family calling circle in MCI's history, your relationship probably is not going to last. Or if you prefer a man who is ambitious and independent, you might want to pass on giving the brother with the squeegee and WILL WORK FOR FOOD sign your telephone number. And yes, sometimes it is hard to tell where a person is coming from until you talk to him for a little while, but nine times out of ten, you can use your spider senses to know when a man is not your type.

They say experience is the best teacher, but I refuse to believe that you should have to sample every piece of rotten candy in the box before you come across the one that doesn't make you gag. Unfortunately, that's exactly what I've had to do, because in the course of my dating career, I have met and dated dumb-jock types, dumber-jock types, Michael Jackson types (they didn't know if they were black or white), and neat freaks. All of whom I had to just say no to. I have also dated men who I thought were perfect for me, and they had to move 20,000 miles away from me to prove that they weren't. However, the men I normally had an allergic reaction to fell into one of six types: the Deodorantly Challenged, the Five and Dime guy, the MeMeMe man (egomaniacs), Thugs, Nice Guys, and those @!#% Dogs.

Waiting to Exhale

I believe that I am a sensible woman. In the past, though, I had reason to question this thinking. For a five-year period, before I wised up, I attracted the kind of men—how can I put this lightly—the kind of men you wouldn't even want to introduce to your Chia pet (yes, I actually own one of those things). Now, I'm not just talking about looks. I'm personally attracted to all kinds of men: attractive, unattractive, high yellow, chocolate mocha, tall, short, even trolls. I am one of those women who has the uncanny ability to find something cute in any man. "Oh, what a lovely shade of green your jagged teeth are." Or "Look at those webbed feet. They must really come in handy at the beach." See? Truly, looks are subjective. Funk, dragon breath, and lice, on the other hand, are not! Believe me, when you think of spending a lot of time with someone, good grooming habits will win out over good looks any day.

Take Carl, for instance. Carl was a nice-looking brother who had what some folks like to call "good hair," but that "good hair" was filled with dandruff the size of corn flakes. Every time I got close to him I had the urge to pour a bowl of milk on his head and go to town. The man thought Head and Shoulders was the latest dance craze. He was in denial because he thought being fine was enough, and for some women who don't mind feeling like it's snowing every time they have sex, it was. I left Carl a case of Denorex and a Dear John letter telling him to wash his hair three times a day with the green stuff and call me when he stopped shedding.

For some men the concept of personal hygiene is just that: a concept. They will go to the gym and play three hours of basketball, lift weights, wrestle in mud with the fellas, and then take a short cut through the sewer to your house, and right before they ring your doorbell they slap on some cologne, thinking they're good to go. Once you open the door they're smelling like that skunk Pepe Le Pew.

"Ugh, what's that smell?"

"Musk, baby."

"I know you *musk* go take a bath!"

Men, you need to wash your ass. That's the bottom line. No funk intended. You might think that you're the bomb, when really you're the stink bomb. Bath & Body Works is not a place where you buy toilet seats and auto parts, and Speed Stick is not a new Olympic sport. Bathing or showering only on special occasions is unacceptable.

Some men, I guess, are just missing that hygiene chromosome. When that is the case, we have an obligation to let these men know that they shouldn't associate stinkiness with being macho. Because women associate stinkiness with, well, stinkiness. We think if your body is stinking, then you have probably left your mark on everything you've touched. We wonder how often you change your drawers. Or what kind of house you keep. And is it safe to eat there? I will always remember this one friend of mine who never missed an opportunity to be funky. He had so much crust on his neck, people mistook him for a pot pie. And he had so much wax buildup in his ears that people would give him money thinking they were at the wax museum. I went over to his house and he asked if I would help him change his sheets. I obliged. Do you know he just turned them over to the other side? The same with his pillows. Talk about nasty.

Dandruff and poor bathing habits are one thing, but halitosis is a whole other animal. Unlike dandruff, which overworks your sense of sight, halitosis messes with your sense of smell and possibly your sense of taste if you dare to kiss a man whose breath smells like he farted through his mouth. I was out with this guy once and when he opened his mouth the smell of stank drawers and rotten eggs enveloped me. My eyes popped out of my head like that *Roger Rabbit* flick, and I could have sworn the hairs on my nostrils were singed. A bad case of halitosis was in the house! We were in a movie theater at the time, so I immediately excused myself and headed for the concession stand. "Give me some licorice, Starburst, Raisinets, Goobers, Junior Mints, and a large Mountain Dew." He refused them all. "If I eat that junk, I'll spoil my appetite." Mine was already spoiled. I held my breath until I almost passed out. Finally I said, "You know, your breath is really kickin'!"

"Aw, baby, I know, but don't hold it against me because I got a bad digestive tract. I can't help it if I got stomach problems." Stomach problems? If it was just the stomach that caused bad breath, hell, get a damn stomach transplant! Baby, it was more than stomach problems—try throat, mouth, and teeth problems.

Men, if a woman offers you a Tic Tac, a stick of gum, a swig of mouthwash, or breathalyzer every five seconds, or if she squints up her nose when you talk or turns her face in another direction—*yo breath stinks*. Halitosis is a force not to be reckoned with. It is a disease that affects millions of people each year and just like with most diseases in the black community, when it hits us, it hits hard.

Just like the brothers who are still walking around with gheri curls (most of whom, for some odd reason, all live in Cleveland), many black men are in denial about halitosis and will add to the problem by refusing to brush their teeth or by insisting that we accept them as they are—stank breath and all. *No!* I'm not having it. Now we may put up with wandering eyes, raggedy rides, and premature ejaculations, but stank breath is asking a little too much. I soon realized that a travel-size bottle of Scope can be a woman's best friend on a bad breath date.

Kim, how do you tell a man he has stank breath without hurting his feelings, you ask? Well, of course you don't come straight out with it, especially if you hardly know him. Try something like, "The smell of a Scope-breathed man really turns me on. Care to gargle?" Now if you don't want to make the wrong impression, I find the best thing to do is bust out the Scope right when the odor is a problem, take a swig for yourself, spit it out and say, "A little dab will do ya," and hand it over to him. If that ain't a hint and a half for his ass, I don't know what is. And remember women, "Keep Scope alive!"

"Sistah, Can You Spare a Dime" Guy

Marvin and I had been dating for about three months when he asked me to go with him to get his mother a birthday present. I thought this was a pretty significant step in our relationship because I felt it meant that meeting his family had to be just around the corner—and we all know when a man wants you to meet his family, he's either really serious about the relationship or he's trying to tell you you're his long-lost sister who was given up for adoption. More important, I was happy that he thought enough of me to want to take me with him. I figured from our conversations and from the way he complimented me that he knew I had good taste and he probably thought I could find the perfect gift for his mother.

I waited with anticipation for him to pick me up as I strategized the gift-buying expedition. I figured he wouldn't know what to buy her so I thought maybe we could start in the perfume department, thinking she would appreciate a nice fresh fragrance to welcome the new season in. Not having a clue about her scent, however, I thought perhaps it would be better if we started in the clothing department, where a nice silk blouse or even a sporty vest might be nice. I just as quickly abandoned that idea when I realized I didn't know the woman's size. For all I knew she bought all her clothes from Tents R Us. Then I thought maybe Marvin would know her taste and we could pick out something quaint that she could use in her home.

Marvin caught me daydreaming as he pulled up in a four-by-four truck I hadn't seen before.

"Hey, Kim. You ready? Why are you so dressed up? Baby, them three-inch pumps aren't going to do. Go put on some sneakers. And put on some jeans."

"Well, all right. A man who is a serious shopper. You're right. I do want to be comfortable." So after changing my clothes, I climbed in the truck and prepared for our shopping outing.

"Okay, so where do you want to go?" I said. "We can go to Manhattan or drive out to some outlet stores where you can catch some really great sales—" Then I noticed that he had begun to slow the truck to a crawl. "Marvin, sweetie, you're driving so slowly the stores will probably be closed by the time we get there."

"Sshh. I think I saw one in the bushes," he said, as if we were crossing enemy lines and he had spotted the attacker. Just great, I thought to myself. The man was having flashbacks from the week he spent in Desert Storm.

"All I see is a dog that looks like he's got the mange. Am I missing something?" I said.

"Here, take this piece of steak and hand me that net between your feet. Get out real slow and try to get him to come to you."

"I didn't know that was your dog. That dog has been roaming the neighbor—"

"Run, Kim. Grab him!"

Before I knew what was happening Marvin had tackled the poor dog, thrown the net over him, and put him in the back of the truck. "Girl, next time I take you shopping with me, you're going to have to be a little quicker. Now grab that red ribbon out of the glove compartment. How good are you at tying a bow?"

I cursed him out under my breath all the way home. He called me a week later and asked me why I hadn't called him.

"I have to be honest with you, Marvin. I thought that was kind of cheap."

"See, that's what's wrong with women," he scolded. "After I washed him up that dog was just like new. You all don't appreciate nothing. It was the thought that counts."

"Okay, so I guess I'll remember you as the guy with the insane thought rather than a cheap-ass man with no shame," I wanted to say. Instead I said, "Come on, this was your mother. Your mother whom you supposedly cherish and love and would do anything for, and you couldn't go out and get her a nice gift?"

"It was from the heart."

"It was from the gutter," I reminded him, and hung up.

Okay, so I shouldn't have hung up on him, and maybe it was even wrong to stop seeing him based solely on that one incident. But let's face it, Marvin gave a whole new meaning to the phrase "finding a bargain." My feeling was if he treated his own flesh and blood like that, I could only imagine the things I would find in my stocking come Christmas. I had a nightmare that I got pregnant and he was the father and he gave me a present in a beautifully wrapped box. When I opened it, it was some hand-me-down cloth diapers.

Don't get me wrong, I don't have the mentality like some

sistahs who think, "He's gotta have it. And I've gotta spend it." I don't measure a man by his bank account or by the amount of money he spends on me. I was raised to take care of myself and not to have to depend on a man for any kind of support, much less financial support. Personally, a lot of times when a man asks me out, I offer to pay or at least go dutch just because I think that's fair. Plus I hate to be beholden to a man—you know, he spent money on me so now he wants to be holdin' on to my thigh.

But I'm not going to lie; every once in a while I like to be pampered. Every now and then I like buying the brand name instead of a generic. And every now and then, I like to valet park just to avoid the hassle. So I don't think it's too much to ask for a man to send me roses or take me out to a nice restaurant every now and then. Now, I'm not talking about the brothers who may have fallen on hard times and just can't afford to, or are not in a position to give you all that your heart desires. I'm speaking to those men who would rather go on a hunger strike than spend an extra dime on you. A guy who watches his pennies like he watches a dancer at a strip club. Those are the kind of men whom I really have very little tolerance for.

I had a friend, Vernon, bless his little frugal heart. He took a job with Nabisco just so he could get free goods. I'd go over to his house and he'd have a cupboard stocked full of cookies and crackers. "Take all you want, Kim."

"Thanks for your generosity," I would tease.

Vernon was so cheap he rigged two bullhorns on each side of his 13-inch television to create the surround-sound effect. He was so proud of his little invention, and he was doubly proud that he'd saved himself some money. "Yeah, them things are expensive. And the price got to come down. Hell, I can wait about six or seven years. In the meantime, this will do." The only ones who seemed to be impressed with his 13-inch "surround-noise" television were the two roaches sitting there, eating popcorn, talking about, "Where's the remote? Turn that shit down a little!"

I should have been suspicious when out of the blue, he told me that he had planned a romantic tropical weekend getaway and that I should pack an overnight bag. I couldn't help but get kind of excited, wondering what little romantic spot he had picked out for us. I packed my swim gear and a couple of cute little sun dresses, and went to his house as he instructed. Standing in the doorway was his fat cousin, Lulu, in a tutu, surrounded by fake, potted banana trees where his couch used to be, beach blankets laid out on the floor, stuffed monkeys hanging from the ceiling, and Bob Marley's "No Woman, No Cry" playing in the background.

"Welcome to Vernon's Village," his cousin said in a bad fake Jamaican accent. *"Vernon! Kim's here. I did it okay. Now give me five dollars. I'm outta here.* Oh yeah, relax, enjoy, and have a pleasant stay. Peace, I'm out."

"Hey, Kim, girl. Ain't this the bomb?" Vernon said, entering from the kitchen, "You don't have to say nothing, the look on your face says it all. I know ain't nobody ever done nothing like this for you before."

"Vernon, why does your cat have black stripes painted across his back?"

"That ain't no cat, that's a vicious tiger, baby girl. Now just relax. I want you to put on your bathing suit. I'm going to rub some suntan lotion on you, turn off the lights, turn on this heat lamp, and I'm going to put in this travel video on Jamaica I rented from Blockbuster. We're going to have a nice romantic getaway just like I promised. And guess what? The video ain't due back till Monday!"

Mama said there'd be days like this . . . but this was ridiculous!

Ten Ways to Tell if a Brother Is Tight

1. For dinner he tells you that you have a choice between the Happy or the Combo Meal.

2. He agrees to drive but insists you reimburse him for gas.

3. Instead of a wallet he carries a piggy bank.

4. The rain is his car wash.

5. He thinks cubic zirconia is a girl's best friend.

6. He doesn't want a raise 'cuz they'll take out more taxes.

7. He buys his groceries and clothes from the same store.

8. 1-800-CALL-COLLECT is his calling-card number.

9. He quit his $50,000-a-year job to join the army so he won't have to pay rent.

10. When he orders take-out, he calls Meals on Wheels.

Sippin' on Gin and Juice

An Ode to the Boyz in the Hood
Oh, my darling Boyz in the Hood.
Why are you so misunderstood?

Your pants are baggy and hang real low.

You sport gheri curls or a big afro.

It don't matter, you wear them well.

Cops harass you, think you got drugs to sell.

They think that you are always gang-banging

When all you're really doing is just hangin'.

You act real tough, inside I know you're nice.

On the corner sipping forties, rolling dice.

Whoa! A drive by, you run and hit the deck.

Yeah, secretly we all want a ruffneck.

I am a people watcher. I love to watch people just doing their thing, especially black men from the hood. They are the most fascinating to watch because unlike your everyday brother (I know, from the media you'd believe the boy from the hood *was* the everyday brother), and unlike the brother who works and lives on Wall Street, there is no pretense. These brothers have no shame. You won't catch them fronting. You won't catch them in stuffy business suits, and they have one way of talking—"Ebonically." If a homey asks one of them, "What's up?" he might say, "It's all good. Just chillin'. 'Bout to go get me a forty." If his mom says, "How you doing, son?" He might say, "It's all good. Just chillin'. 'Bout to go get me a forty—Moms." And if the Reverend sees him and asks . . . well, you get the picture. He's just laid back and cool, with the walk to go with it. It's as if the sidewalk in front of him falls down a few inches right when he takes a step.

After seeing *Boyz N the Hood*, this type of man intrigued me so much that I immediately fell in love with their plight and set out to become an around-the-way girl so I could fit in. I patterned my speech after them. "Yo." I was a rebel without a clause—a subjunctive clause, that is. I studied all the black movies ever made about these gang-banging-type men—which seemed to be most of the black movies that get made. I hung out at liquor stores with hopes of getting robbed by one of them. I went to public schools—deeeeeep in da hood. I had a death wish. Inevitably, I met Sugar Bear—my first, and only, ruffneck.

Sugar Bear was the leader of a gang called Tales from the Crypts, I believe, and I actually met him on a street corner in South Central L.A. I saw him limping across the street and immediately rushed to his aid because I thought he was a victim of a drive by, when really he was just walking really cool. He snatched my gold chain from my neck and took off running. I guess he didn't expect me to holler after him, "Hey, here are the matching earrings!" He was defensive at first, but he took the earrings and we ended up talking a while in the squad car on the way to the station. We hit it off when he saw that my colored contact lenses matched his gang apparel. The biggest challenge in our relationship was teaching Sugar Bear to read. I was intent on changing him into a law-abiding citizen, but he only used this new gift for evil. He now knew how to read street signs, so he had an easier time tracking down rival gangs.

I eventually became an embarrassment to him when he learned, like Janet Jackson in *Poetic Justice*, I wasn't a real around-the-way girl. He tolerated the happy faces I spray-painted next to his gang signs on buildings to mark his territory. But when I tried to unite the gangs by sewing uniforms with all of their colors, I guess I crossed the line. I suppose that "We Are the World" crap doesn't fly in da' hood.

Men Women Play

I remember my first nice guy—Kevin Jones. We were in kindergarten. I don't recall if he was smart or fun to be around, but I do remember that he always gave me his milk and cookies at snack time. That meant a lot back then because truthfully, in kindergarten, what more could a man offer you? He laughed at my jokes, carried my crayons and lunch box home for me, and would let me know if my dress was tucked in my panties after I came from the little girls' room. Yeah, Kevin and I were inseparable. That is, until Jesse Banks showed up.

Jesse was a rotten kid. He wreaked havoc on our kindergarten class the first day he got there. He ate dirt, refused to take naps, beat up the boys, teased and felt up the girls, and would do a daily check to see if I was wearing the correct day-of-the-week panties. Remember those? Worst of all, Jesse cussed out our teacher with words we hadn't even learned yet. I guess you could say he had a real problem with authority. It was love at first insult, and I cut Kevin loose faster than it took the network to drop Arsenio after Farrakhan came on his show. Jesse and I became the Bonnie and Clyde of grammar school. We would lie awake at nap time and plan how we were going to bust out of kindergarten and go right to the first grade. We talked about our hopes and dreams. His was to go on the "Bozo" show and get the ball in bucket number seven, so he could win a brand-new ten-speed and sell the parts. Mine, to go to Mr. Rogers's neighborhood and burn that tired gray sweater he wore every day.

Two weeks later Jesse was picked up by the feds and sent to a juvenile home upstate for setting up his own version of Show-and-Tell in the coat room. After two weeks of deprogramming by child psychologists, I was back to my normal self.

I returned to school to beg for Kevin's forgiveness, only to learn that he had transferred to a new school. And what's the moral of this story? Yeah, kindergarten was a bitch for a sistah growing up in the hood, but more important—give the nice guy a chance!

Now I know that's easier said than done. When there are no sparks it usually means there are no flames. And if there are no flames, there's no sizzle. And if there's no sizzle, what's the point? And sure, you can take the advice of your mother who's desperate for you to get married and get out of her house. "You can learn to love him," she says. I don't know about you, ladies, but sometimes there ain't that much patience in the world. And if we are honest with ourselves, we know that we don't like the nice guys because the nice guys don't provide us with a challenge. They're there when you need them. They're there when you don't need them. They're always on time. They give you what you want, when you want it, with no grief or hesitation. They call when they said they would. They laugh at your jokes. They tell you you're the most beautiful woman in the world. They defend your honor. They give their lives for yours in a second . . . Wait a minute . . . now what's wrong with the nice guy? Oh yeah, he doesn't provide the *umph!* that's needed in a relationship to make it exciting.

Lots of ladies would much rather have a ruffneck than a nice guy. Why is that? Because we are crazy. They are unstable, undependable, carry mucho baggage, and are often dangerous. Hey, there it is! Those of us who push those sweet nice guys to the side are really looking for someone to tame. Come on, admit it, what an accomplishment if we can rope him and tie him down. Nobody ever wants to ride the docile pony at the county fair. You want to ride the wild bucking bronco at the rodeo. (Please, get your mind out of the gutter.)

You want to be the one to tell the world that Sam was a sonofagun when you met him, but now look at him. He's all shaved clean and forming complete sentences and guess what, he doesn't rob 7-Elevens anymore.

After all the scars heal (emotional and sometimes even physical), nice guys start looking real nice and you begin to realize challenges were meant for crossword puzzles and tugs-o-war. I just hope as we grow older, we will begin to love and appreciate ourselves more and recognize that we are deserving of a loving, kind-hearted, nice guy. So hang in there, nice guys! Didn't your mother ever teach you patience was a virtue? It's worth the wait. Oh, and to Kevin, wherever you are, I hope you forgive me, and I hope you're happy!

Man in the Mirror

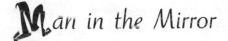

I love a confident man. One who is self-assured, self-reliant, self-basting (OOPS! Sorry, that's a turkey. It must be lunch time), and secure with his physical appearance so that when he strides into a room everyone kind of pauses and stares as if Scottie Pippen walked into the room with a black woman. *Oh no, I didn't go there.* I just get a tingle down my back when I see a man like that. Normally, I just admire them from the table I've crawled under because I'm too embarrassed to cross paths with them. Honestly, they intimidate me because I automatically think they have some X-ray glasses on, and when they look at me they can see all of my shortcomings.

I've come to realize that men like that are just like the beautiful sistah who doesn't have a man because everybody assumes she's already spoken for. *(Yeah, I get a lot of that.)* Men who are confident usually face the same dilemma. Now keep

in mind, I'm talking about confident, not over-confident or conceited men. I bear no man malice if he is sure of himself. In
fact, it is vital to the health and wealth of any man who wants
to go anywhere in life. However, conceited men fall into a
whole other category.

You know those vainglorious, egotistical, smug m.f.ers?
They are the men I am allergic to. They are the men who
know they're the shit and know everybody else knows they're
the shit, and so they start acting like shit. Shit stinks, but it
doesn't know it smells. You know what I mean? The egomaniac is easy to spot. He toots his own horn whenever he
gets the chance. He takes longer to get ready in the morning
than a woman. He irons his T-shirts. He's the kind of man
who will bring a camera on a date and ask you to take pictures . . . of him.

I say never date anyone prettier than you. That leaves out
all the Sylvers and the DeBarges (remember the seventies?).
Ladies, I know we do like a well-groomed, clean cut man. But
I don't want to be cuddling up to no brother who smells or
looks like a French whore (unless it is Dennis Rodman). I know
that not all good-looking men are full of themselves, but be-
ware of the man who stays in the bathroom longer than you.
If you are dating a "pretty boy" you might want to check your
supply of hair-care and skin-care products and just try to get
equal time in the mirror.

Paul was the ultimate egomaniac. Paul and I were in an
acting class together. I didn't really notice him that first day. I
mean, except for the fact that he was tall, handsome, and bow-
legged, had impeccable taste in clothes, kept his fingernails
squarely shaped and closely trimmed, and his dreads well
groomed. But other than that, I didn't give him a second
thought. Well, the first day he decides to introduce himself to

me. Instead of holding out his hand to greet me, he offered me a headshot. "I'm Paul."

"Hi. I'm, um—Kim. Yeah, that's it."

"Oh, don't worry about it. I have that effect on all the ladies. You know, I noticed you are a pretty good actor."

"Oh, thank you. So are you."

"Well, yeah. I do all right. You know, I just finished wrapping a movie with Angela Bassett. Yeah, she asked me to give her some acting tips, so I ended up being her personal acting coach for the movie. I was only supposed to be in one scene, but I delivered the lines so powerfully they rewrote the whole damn movie over and made me one of the principals. But I don't know if it will ever get released because the director was really jealous of me. So the movie probably won't be coming out anytime soon. But yeah, I've been acting since I was delivered into this world. Most people have no recollection of their birth, but I do and I remember when the doctor slapped my behind and I didn't cry. And for some reason, I felt like I better pretend to or else he was going to keep whipping my ass. So yeah. I've been acting a long time. I went to school with Laurence Fishburne. Yeah, he played my understudy in *Raisin in the Sun* in college. Speaking of college, I have a B.A. in blah . . . blah . . . blah."

I thought he would never shut up. I felt like I was listening to one of those annoying car alarms while at the same time opening up one of those gift boxes where you find another smaller gift box, and when you open that one, you find yet another smaller gift box. And then you come to the final gift box, there's not a damn thing in it. That's how I felt as this brother went on and on about himself. The sun could have fallen and risen again, and we would have been standing in the same spot had I not thought of a clever out.

"Paul, I have to go now. See ya." I dropped that acting class, sent his picture and a phony secret admirer note to this girl I could not stand, and went on about my merry way. Life's too short to try and wade through all the bullcrap. And everything he said could have been the truth, but the fact that he felt that I needed to know all that information about him within the first ten minutes of meeting him told me a lot.

If you have a conversation with someone you are meeting for the first time and the only thing you know about the person when the conversation is over is that he or she is a good listener, then that should be a clue that you were a little bit on the loquacious side—you talked too damn much!

Eight Comebacks to Knock "Mr. Thinks-He-Got-It-Going-On" Down to Size

1. Here, let me wipe your mouth. Your gloat is dripping.

2. Wow, if your other head is as big as the one on your shoulders, you must be very uncomfortable.

3. That's a nice suit. I just saw one just like it at Kmart.

4. Are you related to Keenan Ivory Wayans?

5. Oh, I'm sorry, what did you say? I stopped listening the second time you told me you were Mr. Wonderful.

6. Did Sears have a sale on egos today?

7. Did you audition for that new commercial "Let go my ego"?

8. Why don't you and *you* get married. You seem very happy together!

Naughty by Nature

Webster defines "dog" as "a highly variable domestic mammal closely related to the common wolf." Let me offer a nineties' definition: "A male who cheats, lies, steals, and whose only purpose in life is to wreak havoc on an unsuspecting or, most often, suspecting, innocent woman who falls for his crap 99 percent of the time because she's lonely and would rather have a dog than a bone." Is that about accurate? I don't know, though I think these men give canines a bad name. Just think about it. I mean, who doesn't like their pet dog? Pet dogs are adorable and obedient and rarely do they leave the house and not come back for several weeks. Seldom does your pet dog have to go to the vet for an untreated case of gonorrhea. And rarely do you have to call the feds to track down your pet dog to get child support. The only thing that canines and these men-dogs have in common is the need to chase the "cat." And I don't think that's a good enough reason to denigrate canines. A snake or even a praying mantis would be a better metaphor for these creatures who make us want to call Dr. Kevorkian when they're through with us. Come to think of it, even snakes and praying mantis have something these men don't have—it's called a heart. So since there seems to be no name that adequately describes them, and since we have done an injustice to canines everywhere by associating them with these lowlifes, from now on let's start referring to them as "Men Who Give Dogs a Bad Name."

Getting involved with these men is the same as walking into a tornado that has your name on it: Before you know it, you'll be ripped apart and won't know if you're coming or going. What is it about these bad boys that makes us women lose our senses? Maybe it's because they start out being so unpredictable. And I don't care what anybody says, excitement wins over the mundane and the obvious, at least in the beginning, any day. They say they'll call you in a day or so; they call you sometime that decade. They make mad passionate love to you and tell you they love you and no one else, then sleep with your sister. It's like riding a roller coaster. It's thrilling, scary, and exciting all at the same time. What a rush! After you ride it once, you want to get back on and ride it again. After 30 or so trips on that roller coaster, it starts getting really old. And you start analyzing the situation. You realize that it's hot, you're dehydrated, you're dizzy, and this is your 31st time waiting around for a ride that only lasts about 20 seconds. You start to ask yourself, is it really worth it?

I'd like to tell you of a little three-year ride I took once. There was this man at the gym who would stare at me every time I saw him. I got a little uncomfortable because I wasn't sure if I just looked ridiculous in my oversized workout clothes or if he might be an obsessed fan, so I thought I'd ask the manager to talk to the police about this guy. Much to my embarrassment, he *was* the police. As time went by, he began his interrogation. "How are you today? . . . Have you been working your triceps? They sure are looking mighty defined. . . . Hey, I read in *Ebony* that you're separated, is that right?" My sixth sense said run from this nosy sonofagun, so I kept a pleasant distance. "I'm doing well. . . . Thanks, I've worked out real hard today. . . . Yes, I'm separated, but I'm not looking to date right now. Bye!"

Now it is important to note that this brother had two things going for him. The first one was that he had the body of a *god*. I mean the kind of body that just makes you drool. You name it, he had it, and it was in the right place, at the right proportions, and it was HUGE. But when he asked me out, his approach was all wrong. He tried to put on all of this damned intensity. You know the type: While looking deeeeeeply into my eyes (what the hell are you, an optometrist or something?) he said in his best bass profundo voice (that's somewhere between Barry White and Darth Vader), "I have been looking for you, I believe you might be the one." The one what? The one to reject your corny ass. The other thing that he had going was the fact that he was persistent. Believe it or not, he chased me for two years, and believe it or not, he wore me down. What can I say, he was a Taurus to the bone   stubborn and earthy like me, a Capricorn.

One day I thought, I've given every other loser a chance, why not this one? Maybe he'll turn out to be a winner. What did he say to convince me, you ask? "You have probably given a lot of losers a chance. Why not give me a try? I may turn out to be a winner." We had a first date and something happened. I don't know if my braids were too tight (they were freshly done, with more synthetic hair than anybody should have on her head) or if it was the story of how he had raised his daughter on his own after he and his first wife had broken up. I thought, How noble, how brave, a proud black man with a sense of responsibility. Hey, a winner! Yeah, so I'm a sucker for a good story.

After that, it was on, and I'm not embarrassed to say that the sex was phenomenal, although I would be embarrassed if you found out that he growled during the act and I loved it!! There were few demands. I didn't cook. He didn't care. I was busy working a lot, he was working a lot. We saw each other when we could and somewhere along the line he turned out to be intelligent, driven, and, well, you already know about that growling thang! I fell in love.

That was my first mistake. Although I do believe that he was capable of love, he certainly couldn't verbally tell me so. Maybe he had seen one too many bloody crime scenes, but Officer Brother-man wasn't giving it up. He would shut down. I was intent on saving him, loving him so much that he'd have to open up. Loving him so much that the pain of the mean streets would go away. Loving him so much that I didn't kick him to the curb the first time I found a long blonde straight hair on his shoulder. Or the second time or the third time. I think you get the idea.

"Um . . . honey . . . what the hell is this?" He didn't know how that had gotten there. Maybe it was mine. "No, my hair is black and braided and kinky." Maybe it had gotten there at the gym when he helped another patron with an exercise, who, as he believed he recalled, was white and blonde. What the hell exercise was he assisting her with? Some sort of laying down leg press—*with her legs in the air no doubt*—if you get my drift. And then he shut down. He turned back on when I finally got the courage to step. Why take this abuse? He finally told me he loved me, but he waited too long. And never would admit to the evidence I found.

I don't need to tell you how mad a sistah gets when she gets cheated on, but long blonde hairs take the freaking cake. Ya'll saw *Waiting to Exhale*. 'Nuff said. Oh yeah, I forgot to tell you (and you'll never believe) his nickname: Testosterone. Swear to the heavens above. Testosterone. I should have seen it coming. Growl and all.

I was watching "National Geographic" the other day when they had a special on rats. In some cities like Venice, Italy, the rat population is so great that instead of trying to get rid of the rats they have decided to live in harmony with them. This is what I propose. These men who give dogs a bad name are here and they are not going anywhere. They are our brothers, fathers, cousins, uncles, preachers, foot specialists—yes, I dated a dog who was a foot specialist. The best thing you can do is be prepared. Learn to identify them, befriend them, commune with them, but don't fall in love with them!

Ten Sure-fire Ways You Can Tell if Your Man Is a Dog

1. He calls and tells you he's working late, but he hasn't had a job since the Supremes broke up.

2. He gives you a set of keys to his house, but he lives in an apartment.

3. You've just made mad passionate love and he tells you he wants to marry a virgin.

4. He is the president of the Rick James Fan Club.

5. He believes the world is going to end soon, so there is no reason to discuss your future.

6. You can't have his home number because he's a Black Panther.

7. His ideal romantic evening includes you, him, and his wife.

8. There are revolving doors installed in his bedroom.

9. He asks you to marry him after your doctor announces you have two months to live.

10. He wants to set the wedding date for the month after December and the month before January.

Now see, men, that wasn't so bad was it? Some of you will walk away saying, "Okay, so Kim thinks we're heartless, funky, lazy, cheap, hard, arrogant wimps. What are you complaining about?" I never said all men were this way. But if the shoe fits . . . it's your shoe. I can hear it now. "First *Waiting to Exhale* and now this. That's why black men can't get a break. The man won't let us get ahead. They paint us as the perpetrator time after time on the news. They make us look weak in movies, and now Kim, the one person who I thought had our backs, is doggin' us. What's a brother to do?"

All I can tell you is to keep reading, my brother, because it's going to get worse before it gets better. I'm just kidding. Do I have to remind you that this is a book meant to delight? I have an equally long laundry list of the things I love about black men. The problem is my dog ate that list, so I had to go with what I had. You know what I'm saying? I'm *teasing*!!! Read on.

Weird Science

♥ I was strolling through the park one summer day when out of the blue he appeared. When our eyes met, a feeling that I had never experienced before engulfed my entire being and I knew that this was the man I had been looking for all of my life. We introduced ourselves with our eyes. I could feel him taking in every part of me. His eyes told me he too had been searching for me all of his life, and now with great pleasure and a quiet anxiety he knew his search was over.

He gently took my hand, touching it as if it were a fragile newborn baby. He passed over every line, every groove, every cuticle like each distinct part made him feel and understand who he had dreamed I would be. Then he held me, instinctively realizing that I was not a dream, and we both grew excited as we anticipated the wonderful life that was in store for us now that we had found each other.

We spent the next three days getting to know each other. He had a brilliant mind to go along with his flawless body. We discussed the great African kings and queens, and he spoke of Zaire and Egypt and other African lands as if they were heaven. We rapped about Plato and Socrates and all the great poets and artists of their time. We laughed a lot. He marveled at the genius of Richard Pryor and Redd Foxx and reflected on Dick Gregory. And he asked my opinion.

He intently listened to me as I vented my frustrations about my job and other parts of my life that I was not pleased with. He held me while I cried and never once did he attempt to judge or offer solutions, for he knew what I needed at that moment. When I finished pouring out my soul, he kissed my eyelids as if to take the sadness away and comforted me until I felt all was right with the world again. He painstakingly gathered flowers for me, making sure that each one was a reflection of his feelings for me. He recited love poems that sounded as if they had come from the core of his soul. Every time he looked at me he told me I was beautiful and he kissed me as if he were kissing me for the first and last time.

He confessed that he wasn't a good cook but he offered to make me dinner. He studied cookbooks as if they were the Bible itself. And he prepared a simple but elegant meal and fed it to me. We made passionate love. Our bodies glided in the rhythm of the darkness. He was gentle and loving, and we simultaneously exploded into deep ecstasy. Our bodies quivered ever so peacefully as we floated back down to the softness of the bed. Then he took me into his arms and looked into my eyes and said, "I thank God for you," and told me I was beautiful and held me all night long.

This man had discovered the password to my heart and entered cautiously, knowing exactly what I needed and how to give it to me. He was my protector, my confidant, my lover, he was the most perfect creature on this earth.

And then I noticed the antennas. Two little antennas protruding from the top of his head. He had been sent to earth to study humans, he explained, and had stumbled upon me in the park. He could barely mouth the words, but then he confessed that he had "phoned home" and his superiors demanded that he return immediately. We made love one last time. We cried and caressed each other and I drove him to his spaceship. I cried all the way home, but felt some comfort in knowing that I now had the answer to the question that so many of my friends and I had been asking for the last several years. "Where are all the good men?" I knew exactly where they were, and the next morning I was going to get my butt down to NASA and sign up for that space program.

Black women have it rough, don't we? You finally meet the perfect man and he turns out to be a brother from another planet.

Creating the Perfect Man

What if we could assemble a team of female scientists to create the perfect man? You would have sisters lined up around the block. Of course they wouldn't be going for those average, everyday brothers—they gots to get paid and they wants to be seen, so they're going for the celebs and the athletes. With Denzel's (good God!!) good looks, combined with Michael Jordan's bank account, Jim Brown's integrity, that model Tyson's body, Laurence Fishburne's intensity, Wesley Snipes's suave demeanor, Malik Yoba's um, um, well anything Malik would like to donate would be graciously accepted, L L Cool J's raw sex appeal, Will Smith's boyish charm, Duane Martin's cutie-pie-ness, Barry White's vocals, Heavy D's sensitivity, Jesse Jackson's ability to rhyme everything he says, and Dennis Rodman—you know he's got to have a little freak in him. Just imagine what male specimen you would have concocted: an irresistible, fine, intelligent, kinky, Tone Loc? Come to think of it, he would probably be conceited and arrogant as hell because he'd know all the women wanted him. Okay, maybe this mixing of genes wouldn't be such a good idea.

The Oven of Lovin'

Have you ever thought about how a man is like food? He can be tasty, nutritious, filling, and sometimes can make you nauseous, especially if he stays out all night.

I have a secret recipe that has been in my family for years. So far I haven't been able to perfect the dish, probably because I've been having trouble finding all of the right ingredients. Why don't you give it a try? The recipe is on the next page.

The Man Formerly Known as a Prince

I don't want to sound too demanding, but is it really wrong to want the perfect man? Well, maybe it is demanding and unrealistic, but it is not my fault. And if you feel like me, don't you blame yourself either. The blame lies with the Brothers Grimm and all the others who created those damn fairy tales. Our well-meaning mothers read all those stories to us at bedtime and we would go to sleep dreaming of Cinderella and Snow White and Sleeping Beauty, believing that someday our prince would come too. He'd be rich and handsome and gallant and all of that. The problem is that poor poor Cindy, Snowy, and Sleepy-Head were all victims. They sat around being sad, misused little creatures who needed someone to either awaken them with kisses or help them find their shoe. So all these little girls get indoctrinated with these dangerous notions that if you are unhappy enough and beautiful enough and suffer enough, some fine man will come and sweep you off your feet, change your life, and

Recipe for the Fantastic Fellow

♥

A tasty treat to be devoured or nibbled on anytime, and the best part of all is, you can gorge yourself on this savory feast and not gain any weight.

1 190-lb., 6' man

1 cup of compassion

1 cup of sensitivity

dash of good looks

2 cups of kindness

6 oz. sense of humor

bunch of bravery

1 pint of honesty

2 tablespoons of spirituality

spoonful of sugar
(makes the medicine go down)

pinch of good sense

32 white teeth

1 bushel of money

2 hard-working hands

6–8" love sausage, for garnish

bottle of wine, roses, candles, satin sheets (optional)

Take the man, wash carefully, dry, and set aside. Give him a glass of wine and let him marinate. Knead the compassion, sensitivity, good looks, kindness, humor, bravery, honesty and spirituality by hand, softly so as not to bruise. Add sugar to make it sweet and sprinkle all over his body. (Note: If you add too much sugar, he may be a little too "sweet"). Beat good sense into his head. Affix the teeth. Take the bushel of money and set up a joint bank account. Then attach two hard-working hands in an open, giving gesture (kinda like the Allstate hands). Cut the love sausage to size, affix, and season to taste (Ah, suki suki now!). Light the candles. Coat the sheets with rose petals, fold lightly, and lay your sexy snack on top of a bed of satin sheets. Jump in, heat it up, and get cookin'. Bon appétit!

you'll live happily ever after. Sometimes fairy tales do come true like the song says, but how many brothers do you know who ride around on white horses saving damsels in distress? (White Cadillacs maybe, but that sounds like a pimp, not a prince.)

Yeah, well, dream on, Rapunzel, the men (and you know they were men) who wrote these fairy tales centuries ago didn't take into account that women are strong. Sometimes society would have you believe otherwise, but we know the deal. Empower thyself. It sure would be nice if Mr. Right came along, but if that didn't happen, Cinderella could've packed up her rags in bags and run away from that bitch of a stepmother and dem two dog-faced stepsisters. After all, she had a fairy godmother, why didn't she just ride that pumpkin-coach to someplace like the Grand Cayman Islands, trade those uncomfortable glass shoes for a pair of sandals, and just chill? Snow White (Is her name a description of her virtue? Or maybe she just needed some sun . . .) could've taken those happy, sleepy, and grumpy, etc., little boys and started a rap group called S W and the 7 D's. They would've toured and made some serious dough. *Hi Ho ya'll, Hi Ho ya'll, to da beat ya'll, she's a freak ya'll.* And as for poor Sleeping Beauty, well I have to admit that I always had problems with this one. Even as a kid, I was able to read the underlying metaphor of a woman needing a man to "awaken" or enlighten her, as it were. That and the fact that I truly worried about her. All I could ever think about was how bad her morning breath must've been after being asleep for 100 years. Yuck. I was an intense kid, huh?

Now I don't want to bring you down or damn you to the life of a spinster, I just want to offer another theory on why we set our standards so high. In my opinion, movies, romantic novels, and soap operas all have an enormous influence on the psyche of women. We spend our time indulging in these activities and fantasizing about why we can't meet any men like that, or worse, why our current man isn't like that. Don't we hate it when men look at the *Sports Illustrated* swimsuit issue or the Playboy Channel and then look over at us and wonder why our thighs aren't that small, why our breasts aren't that big, or why we can't do *that* with our tongue? It simply is not fair.

In one romance novel you might read about some young beautiful heiress named Hillary whose golden tresses flow in the wind. One day while out riding her prize-winning stallion, she stops in a green meadow and meets a stranger who is practicing his archery. The stranger is mysterious and handsome and has the body of a Greek god. She watches him quietly from behind a tall oak tree. Hillary becomes startled and screams when a squirrel scampers across her delicate toes, causing her to trip over some pinecones. *I know, I know, she is standing under an oak tree, but pine smells so good, doesn't it?* Anyway, this disturbance causes the handsome archer to notice her. Her exceptional beauty causes him to miss his target and mistakenly hit a duck that just happened to be waddling by at that moment. As luck would have it, they were both hungry, so he asks Hillary to lunch. The archer builds a fire to cook the duck, and the two of them sit and eat and fall in love and share greasy kisses for the rest of the afternoon. *Come on, everyone knows how fatty duck meat is.*

Silly, isn't it? Well of course it is, because the women reading this crap are probably not going to have an experience like this. Oh please, how many brothers do you know who are into archery? My point is that this stuff is dangerous. We read of this magic perfect stuff of dreams and then compare our lives to it, and we come to the conclusion that our relationships are dull, unromantic, and uninteresting.

If you are looking for Mr. Right, you may have to come to terms with the fact that he simply might not exist. Why? Because nobody is perfect, and saying that you are searching for

Mr. Right is way too much pressure. Try looking for someone who is right for you instead. Sometimes you just have to admit that it's so rough out there that you may have to settle. I'm not suggesting that you date anything because you are lonely and desperate, but let's face it, you may need to compromise. Here is a handy chart to help you analyze and intellectualize your way to a healthy, albeit rationalized, relationship.

Mr. Right ♥	Mr. Right Now ♥
He's soft-spoken.	He doesn't yell during every argument.
He's rich.	He knows the billing cycle on all of his eighteen credit cards.
He has a nice car.	He knows exactly where to park his car so the repo man won't find it.
He's tall.	He doesn't mind wearing heels like Prince.
He's upwardly mobile.	He has a job.
He's ambitious.	He has a job.
He can please you sexually.	He doesn't fall asleep right away.
He has a great sense of humor.	He knows a couple of knock-knock jokes.

Oh, Romeo . . .

I have always fallen for guys who could romance me. Jerod was my kind of man when it came to romance. We met years ago when I was still doing stand-up in New York. On one of our first dates, he had a limo pick me up and he asked me to dress formally for the occasion. He might as well have said wear a space suit 'cuz you know sistahs ain't got a whole lot of formal wear in their closets. The choice was between an old prom dress and a fuchsia bridesmaid gown. The prom dress had somehow miraculously shrunk (isn't it funny how clothes have a tendency to do that?) and that big wide fuchsia bow wasn't doing anything for me, especially in the back. So I went to Macy's with a quickness. The limo driver was prompt and drove me to a fabulous restaurant in Manhattan where my Don Juan of the ghetto was waiting outside in the pouring rain, in the winter, on one knee, with a single red rose, singing a ballad that he had written just for me. I will never forget that day, or Jerod. He came down with pneumonia two days later, but what's important to remember is that despite his illness, he had made me happy. After Jerod, I told myself I would never ever date a man who wasn't romantic. So you can probably guess that I sat home a lot.

Sometimes we get what we ask for and realize it ain't all that. Take Ronald. He was another one who could romance the skin off you. On one of our first dates, we had dinner by candlelight on his terrace with a wonderfully romantic view overlooking the ocean. We shared an expensive bottle of champagne from his wine cellar and talked into the wee hours of the night. Then he suggested we each write something about each other on a piece of paper and put it in the empty bottle of champagne. The bottle was to be sealed and not opened until our one-year anniversary. Talk about planning ahead! A man who actually could see me in his future was definitely a positive sign of things to come. NOT!

Don't get me wrong, he continued to romance me during the times in our relationship when we weren't arguing. Remember Paula Abdul's song "Opposites Attract"? Well, Ronald and I were "Opposites Attack." Have you ever been with someone whose dirty drawers you loved, but you argued 24/7? That's how Ronald and I were. We would argue so much, I felt like Newt Gingrich at a pro-choice debate. Our arguments ranged from subjects like whether or not Cuban refugees should be turned away to almost coming to blows over whether Emmanuel Lewis and Gary Coleman were the same person. (Now it was true, you never saw them together, but I'm pretty certain Gary had at least six inches on the E-man.) I hung in there 'cuz, well, he was a romantic and making up, like the song says, was half the fun. Too bad that theory only lasts as long as the song does. After about six months of getting my mental butt whipped, we agreed that it just wasn't working.

It would have been an amicable separation had I not suggested we read the notes we had written to each other and tucked away in the champagne bottle on our first date. He first read my note to him: "Ronald, your wonderful smile was the first thing I noticed about you. I wish many things for our future, and one is that a year from now I will look across from you and still see you smiling." Nice, right? It had come from the heart. Then I read his note: "Kim, you're a psycho bitch and you need to get some help!" Apparently, after one of our more peppered arguments, he got so mad that he tore up the original note and replaced it with that. So, to prove him right I cracked the bottle over his head and ran.

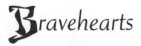

Bravehearts

I love men with muscles. I think it's psychological, but I feel secure when I'm with a man who looks as though he could

slay a lion. I think women want a man who they can really be with *and* feel safe. Why do you think that show "Lois & Clark" is so popular? Women want a man who is masculine like Superman, yet sensitive like Clark Kent. That's every woman's fantasy. Trust me, fellas. No woman wants to go out with a man who is a little bitch. Or a man who expects you to carry *him* over the threshold on the honeymoon. Now that doesn't mean we don't want you to talk about your feelings, and it doesn't mean we don't want to see you cry, because that's all part of being sensitive. But there are definite times and places when we need you to be strong. For example, if I'm out with you and another man starts pawing at me like I'm going to be his last supper, you would want to put the brother in check before I have to. Seriously, if I am with you and you allow another person to come into our space, that is not a good thing. If I have to take off my good pair of pumps and use them to knock the hell out of the crazy man, while you're standing there saying, "Yeah, okay man, okay," you can believe there won't be a second date. Now I know what some of you are thinking: "You want a bodyguard; you don't want no damn man." No, I want a man who I can walk down the street with and not feel like if some fool jumps out to rob us, he's gonna look at me and say, "Kim, get him!"

Mission Possible Man

For as long as I can remember, I have always been attracted to men who were going places. Although, sometimes those places had signs that read ONLY ONE CALL PER PRISONER PLEASE. But I like men who want more out of life than just the simple things. Food, clothing, and shelter are cool, but I'm talking about degrees here. Do you want soup, Sears, and a shack? Or would you rather have Chateaubriand, Calvin Klein, and a condo? I don't want to sound materialistic, but don't we want the best things in life? Oh sure, I can get them for myself and I urge women to strive for themselves, but I sure wouldn't mind a mate who can get there with me.

I remember Dr. Martin Luther King's "I Have a Dream" speech, and the part that really stuck in my mind was the part about whatever you decide to do in life, be the best. You remember: "If you're going to be a street sweeper, be the best street sweeper you can be. . . ."

That was so powerful and it made so much sense. It made me think, "Wow, if I become a street sweeper, what would people say when I died?"

"What did she do for a living?"

"She was a street sweeper."

"Was she any good?"

"Nah. She was just awright."

That would kind of mess with me, so I guess that's why I work hard at whatever I set out to do.

Now, some say men are the laziest creatures on the planet. I don't know how true that is, but I do know that they invented the remote control, microwave ovens, and the wheel. Think about it. At one time, there was no reason to go anywhere because everyone just lived in the same cave. I bet it was a man who was too lazy to chase after Tyrannosaurus Rex on foot, so he invented the wheel. Of course brakes wouldn't be invented for several centuries, so T-Rex probably had some good eatings.

The men who have been in my life while I was growing up followed Dr. King's example. My father, my uncles, my male teachers were all men whom I looked up to because they were hungry and wanted more from life. Now, I don't mean a man who will lie, cheat, or steal to get ahead, or a man who neglects his family. There has to be a balance. I just want a man who follows the dictate of the Army slogan, "Be all that you can be."

Sadly, most of the men I've dated have been lazy as hell. I think there is an invisible lifeguard/paramedic/firewoman sign on my back that reads: ALL NEEDY APPLY HERE. DON'T WORRY, I'LL SAVE YOU. This started back when I was a little girl. I was attracted to the boys no one wanted on their team, or the boys who didn't seem to have enough Legos in their Lego set. If there was a guy in school who was unpopular and needed a date to the school dance, they'd just say, "Ask Kim!" And on top of agreeing to go to the dance, I would have to help him pick his tux, buy my own corsage, and pay the subway fare. I guess I felt a little sorry for them, not to mention I was also getting my community service points for the honor society.

I really felt that once I hooked up with these guys, it was my job to make sure they were okay. Which was fine, when I was 12 and even 17, but as an adult, carrying a grown man on your back kind of wears on you. And I would realize, yeah they're okay, but I'm not okay and that's not okay. Because after a while you get tired of dating a man who comes equipped with his own backpack full of wipes and fresh diapers. And after a while you just want to be with someone who is out on the track of life running right there beside you, instead of somebody you gotta be telling, "Come on, catch up, motherfucker! Run. Catch up!" Or worse yet, somebody who ain't even on the track with you, but sitting up in the bleachers, with a Polish sausage in one hand and a corn dog in the other, hollering, "You go, girl! I'll wait for you at the finish line." I want someone who is going to be there warming up right along with me, getting into position, and who's going to take off when that starter pistol sounds. Someone who is willing to fight the good fight and run the race with me. You know? That's how I had to break it down for the last brother I dated. And you know what his response was? "So, Kim, what you trying to say? I just bought you some Gatorade—I'm there for you, girl."

Call me when you can pull your own weight, and is that too much to ask? And I'm not saying the man has to be making more money than me or have a bigger house or a better car. But it would be nice if at 32 he's not still living at his mama's house and thinking progress is getting his own phone line.

I want me a Colin Powell–Bill Gates–Bill Cosby–Donald Trump–Bryant Gumbel–Bill or Hillary Clinton kind of man. Did you get all of that?

The Good Humor Man

Have you ever had a day where everything that could go wrong did? You know, the kind of day that at the end of it you just wanted to go home and cry?

On top of waking up late, having a bad hair day (you know you're having a bad day when you have hair extensions and you're still having a bad-hair day), getting lost, and blowing an audition, my monthly visitor decided to come by unexpectedly just as I was having my pupils dilated at the eye doctor. That was the kind of day I was having when I met Brian at the grocery store in the personal hygiene aisle. He offered his assistance when he saw me scaling the shelves like Spiderman 'cuz I couldn't see more than two feet in front of me. I thought I would die right there on the spot, but I finally whispered, "Could you please help me find the female products?"

"Oh. I think the hairspray is in the next aisle," he whispered back.

I pleaded with him, "Please, this is an emergency. I need some sanitary products."

"Oh, now I know for sure the bleach is in aisle twelve," he joked. "I'm just messing with you. What you're looking for is right here," he said as he continued to assist me even though I was so embarrassed I could have peed on myself. "Now let's see, do you need the light flow kind or the heavy flow? Oh, they even got super flow. Oh, wait. Better yet, why don't you just do like Toni Braxton and 'Let it Flow'?"

I burst out laughing right there in the store. I mean here I was having the worst day of my life and this man had, for a brief second, made me realize that things weren't that bad by telling a period joke. He made me relax in a situation where I had every right to be tense and uncomfortable. He managed to turn my frown upside down. He was able to make me see that the glass was half full when only seconds before I saw it half empty and leaking fast. He made me laugh. That alone was enough for me to want to take him home, or at least bottle up some of his great attitude and take that home with me.

A man who has a sense of humor scores major points in the game of love with me. I mean life is tough sometimes, and I'd much rather be with a man who can help me put on a happy face than a man who is mad at the world and blames me. I dated a guy who was so angry all of the time, I would get mad just thinking about him.

I like a man who knows the punch line and can deliver it at just the right moment.

"Honey, do you want me?"

"Naw, my little soldier is standing at attention because it thinks it's in the army."

You know, the kind of man who can be around your family, no matter how dysfunctional they are, and still be comfortable. I had a friend who confessed to her boyfriend that her sister was an alcoholic and a habitual liar, as well as neurotic and a kleptomaniac. He responded with, "Do you think she would mind stopping by and cheering up my manic-depressive brother?"

Now I know what some of you are thinking. "Oh, Kim just wants her own personal court jester. Her own clown." Not true. I'm talking about a man who without much effort can see the lighter side of a situation and is not walking around like Schlep Rock all of the time.

When a man is upbeat and in good spirits it's naturally going to make you feel good. Besides being good for the soul, I hear laughter stimulates the same muscle as the orgasm. So think about it. Forget your troubles, come on, get happy!

The Nutty Professor

When I was in high school, I used to have this ridiculous crush on my chemistry professor, Mr. Tidsworth. He wasn't good looking by my standards. And as you know by now, my standards are not that high. He kind of looked like a cross between a frog and Ross Perot. He wasn't personable. His "good mornings" always came out as these really rough grunts, like he was trying to clear a hairball from his throat. But the thing that excited me about Mr. Tidsworth was that he was the smartest man I had ever met. I would look forward to his class every afternoon, listening to his lectures as if they were love poems. "Okay, class, today we are going to be discussing how nitrogen sulfate coagulates with amino acids to cause a catalytic conversion of atmospheric pressure. . . ." I remember wanting to raise my hand and say in my most seductive voice, "Ah, Mr. T, could you repeat that, and a little slower this time."

The man had it going on in the brain department. He rattled off formulas and equations like he was reciting his telephone number. There wasn't a question he couldn't answer. If they had an A list for brains, like they do actors in Hollywood, his name would have been right at the top. Okay, I was a mere kid. I probably thought the school janitor was a genius. I mean, for all I knew, Mr. T could have been trained at the Academy of Idiots and could have been teaching us from his toy chemistry set. A fraud or not, though, one thing Mr. Tidsworth made me realize was that I was attracted to smart men.

I don't measure a man's intelligence by the number of degrees he has. I've known people with Ph.D.s and the only thing they were certain of was that they had a Ph.D. I'm not impressed by the guy who says he knows 103 languages, but has no plans to ever travel out of his home town. What's the point, you know? Or if a guy says he graduated summa cum laude, but his class size was two: him and a guy named Bubba. Men who have a thirst for knowledge but would rather be dehydrated than get off their butts and go learn something, do nothing for me. But, if a man tells me he was a contestant on "Jeopardy"—hell, if he tells me he watches "Jeopardy"—I get excited. More important, a man who loves information and is conversant on different subjects wins my heart every time. I was trying to get this guy I was dating to read a book that I had just finished. I really wanted him to read it so we could discuss it. He told me, "I don't like to read."

At first it didn't compute. "What, you don't like to read at night? You don't like to read fiction? What?"

"Naw, I just don't like to read. It's boring."

That was the biggest letdown. I mean there was a time not too long ago when people were killed for even trying to learn to read.

With a smart man, you don't have to be on your p's and

q's all of the time. If you're lost somewhere, you can relax because you know he's going to find the way. You can't lose because it's almost guaranteed you're going to learn something. After all, I think I'm pretty intelligent my damn self, so a smart man makes me feel like Kim squared! Seriously, I'd take a man who knows the importance of iron and its properties over a man who can pump iron but who talks like Baby Huey any day.

In all sincerity, I think women in general, me included, want someone to love and have that love returned. And getting a puppy isn't the same thing, trust me. If that man happens to be smart, has a little romance in him, can make me laugh, will lay down his life for me, and wants to conquer the world with me by his side, all the better!

Bump trying to come up with a formula or a recipe. A partner; that's what women really want. Someone who respects us, who we can trust, and we know will always be by our side. A partner . . . hmmm. Maybe I should just join the police force.

♥

Dating in the Nineties and Beyond — How to Find Mr. Right On!

I met a guy over the telephone the other day. He sounded nice and chipper and for some reason I was in an unusually good mood. He was going to give me the phone number of a store, but we ended up talking about the meaning of life, sports, and the decline of the Roman Empire. I mean it wasn't like any other conversation I had before. It was amazing how much we had in common: We both lived in the United States and we were both single. The conversation was so stimulating, I began to understand why phone sex was so popular.

After about 35 minutes, I politely reminded him about the number he was supposed to be getting for me. He gave it to me, and I abruptly told him to have a nice day, and hung up. Was that the most foolish thing or what? I don't know, I guess I just got scared, you know? I mean, what if he looked like one of those aliens on Star Trek with the indentation in their heads, or worse: What if his butt was so high, it made Arsenio's ass look normal? I should talk, I've got a high booty too.

I just felt like it was too much pressure. I mean, it's important to be physically attracted to someone first if you're thinking about having a meaningful relationship.

What if he turned out to look like a Gila monster, with a lot more monster in him than Gila? What's a Gila anyway? How do you tell a guy with whom you had a wonderful evening that the conversation was great, the meal was enjoyable, he was a complete gentleman, but that third eye in the middle of his forehead was kind of distracting? How can you be honest about something like that without making him feel bad? "So, Mr. Cyclops, you must take a little extra time at the optometrist?"

I guess that's why blind dates—oops, I mean dates between two strangers arranged by a third party (if you want to be politically correct)—are so terrifying. You don't know what to expect. And I think another reason why people are resistant to going on a blind date is because it seems so unnatural. When I think of meeting "the one," I think of how Humphrey Bogart fell for Ingrid Bergman in *Casablanca*. I think of Antony and Cleopatra, or Elizabeth and Richard, or Diana Ross and Billy Dee in *Lady Sings the Blues*, or Elizabeth and Richard the second time, for that matter. You arrange your closets, you arrange flowers, you arrange an appointment with your dentist, but something just doesn't seem right about arranging destiny.

I think dating in any form, next to public speaking and death, is one of the most feared rituals in this society. You plan an evening with a complete stranger and if you like what you see, you pray to God that this one date will eventually lead, in the near future, to him seeing you naked. Plus, dating feels like an audition; you hope to get picked to co-star in a blockbuster relationship.

I bet if more research was done, it would be found that dating is hazardous to your health. I'm serious. Before you consider dating, I think there should be warning labels posted somewhere. The whole process is just so darn complex. Think about it. First you have to find someone you're attracted to enough to stomach him for a couple of hours, then you have to let him know you're interested in exploring the attraction further, at the same time seeing if he shares your feelings, and most important, you have to find out if he is available. To top it all off, you have to prepare for the date, and then, finally, hope that it was worth the time and effort that went into it all.

And sometimes, just sometimes, you realize the man you're staring at across the table just might have what it takes to advance to the finals, which truthfully is a lot scarier when you think about it. It's like walking into a minefield: You know if you say one dumb thing, you've blown it. Or you might be taken off-guard when he goes to hug you good night and end up giving him a swift kick to the groin. Situations like that could possibly ruin any chance for happiness.

First dates can be especially painful because they can be so darn awkward. Awkward like when you're meeting your gynecologist for the first time and you're both trying to make small talk while he's on his "expedition." Awkward like when you're dissing one of your friends to another friend, and the friend you're dissing happens to be right behind you and hears every terrible thing you say. Awkward like when you lied on your résumé just to get the job, and someone hands you a scalpel and a mask.

Back in the days of our parents and grandparents the dating rules were a lot simpler. Once a woman turned sixteen, she married the closest thing standing next to her. (And if you lived in the Ozarks, it might be your cousin.) The man was the breadwinner, the woman stayed home with the kids, and they stayed married no matter what. So what if you weren't able to develop your own interests and hobbies, or work outside of the home? And so what if your life only revolved around your husband and your children? Okay, so maybe simpler doesn't necessarily mean better.

I wish you could just handle the whole thing like a job interview. You ask him to bring his personal and sexual résumé. You inform him that he will be interviewed by a panel that consists of your parents and your two best girlfriends. In addition, you tell him that there will be no food served, so you don't have to worry about him seeing you chew with your mouth open. Then you ask him to take the following "Let's See if You Can Kick It with Me" Test.

1. What type of relationship are you seeking at this time?
    a. Committed and monogamous (hope it will lead to marriage)
    b. Platonic and casual (fuck buddy)
    c. Someone to pick up where my mother left off
    d. All of the above

2. I pay my bills
    a. each month and on time
    b. when the feeling hits me
    c. with the assistance of a guy named Shorty Smalls
    d. hopefully with the line of credit you will extend me

3. I consider myself intelligent because
    a. I know my telephone number by heart
    b. I have a large head

c. I can guess all the puzzles on "Wheel of Fortune"
    d. I can break into almost any house

4. The last time I took a bath/shower was
    a. this morning
    b. when I noticed my underwear standing in the corner by themselves
    c. when Milli Vanilli was popular
    d. the last time we had a good rain

5. I think women
    a. are bitches and should die
    b. should be seen and not heard
    c. are God's greatest creation
    d. both a and c

6. I like to spend my free time
    a. vegging out on the couch, watching sports, holding my penis
    b. writing love poems to my significant other
    c. vegging out on my friend's couch watching sports, holding my penis
    d. holding my penis

7. When I get married I would like
    a. a small and intimate wedding
    b. a wedding with 200 to 300 of my fiancée's family and closest friends
    c. a prenuptial agreement
    d. a mistress

8. How many children would you prefer?
    a. Two
    b. A busload
    c. I would prefer a puppy or goldfish instead
    d. None, I already have several

9. When my penis is erect, it is
    a. bigger than a dill pickle that comes in those barrels at the grocery store, but smaller than a bread basket

      b. a worm on steroids
      c. at least eight inches
      d. Do you mean before or after I pump up the penile implant?

18. When I make love to my woman, it is important that
      a. she satisfies me
      b. she is satisfied
      c. she is awake
      d. she put a battery in the video camera first

If a man is gainfully employed, has good grooming habits, can carry on a decent conversation, is a gentleman, has an appreciation for women, and is a gentle, thorough lover, with adequate "equipment," then that's pretty much enough for a woman to give a man the time of day. And if they aren't adverse to marriage and children, then hot damn!

Sometimes you just want to fast forward through all the getting-to-know-you crap and feel comfortable enough in front of him so that you can scratch your crotch if it gets a little itch. Unfortunately, the dating ritual is a part of the whole love equation if you're hoping for a meaningful relationship that's going to last longer than Magic Johnson's retirements seemed to.

What sometimes can be harder than the actual date is finding suitable prospects—especially for black women—when we are told day in and day out that over a third of the black male population is in jail, which makes the likelihood of marriage for sistahs as likely as it would be for Mario Van Peebles to make another hit movie.

With this in mind, we have to start being creative in our pursuit of love. If we look at the ways we go about meeting people, no wonder we have such poor results. What else can we really expect? It's a shot in the dark. We spend more time at the grocery store checking our fruit for bruises than we do searching for our soul mate. Let's take a look at some of those ways. Shall we begin?

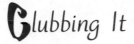lubbing It

At the insistence of my girlfriend, I went out to a nightclub recently. The music was so loud, I thought I was experiencing an emergency broadcast message. I was waiting for someone to come over the loud speaker to say, "This is a test, this is only a test." Of course it never came. Instead, a man in a leopard-printed polyester suit with a 1/2-karat gold tooth sauntered up to me and hollered in my ear:

"DO YOU WANT MY PANTS?"

"NO, THANK YOU, I HAVE A PAIR JUST LIKE THAT AT HOME!"

"NO, I SAID, DO YOU WANT ROMANCE?"

"I THINK YOU'RE BEING A LITTLE FORWARD!!"

"I SAID, DO YOU WANT TO DANCE!!!"

"OH, WHY DIDN'T YOU SAY THAT IN THE FIRST PLACE!!!"

I have to admit, dancing released a lot of the tension that had built up, and after the Macarena, the Bump, and the Electric Slide I really felt I had bonded with my new freaky-fashioned friend. So when he asked if he could come back to my table and buy me a drink, I gave him a thumbs-up. Big mistake.

"SO WHAT'S YOUR NAME, SWEET THANG?"

"PORSCHE." *(My club name.)*

"UH UN. YOU KIM COLES. I SEENT YOU ON THAT SHOW THAT BE COMING ON FOX, 'IN LIVING SINGLES'."

"IT'S 'LIVING SINGLE,' NOT 'IN LIVING SINGLES'."

"SAME THING, SAME THING. SO ANYWAY, MY NAME IS MOHAMMED AKBAR O'MALLEY."

"AND WHAT DO YOU DO FOR A LIVING?"
"LET'S JUST SAY I DON'T STEAL FROM PEOPLE AND I DON'T HURT PEOPLE . . . ANYMORE."

"OH." *Check please.* Where was an earthquake when you needed one? I mean, what do you say after something like that? Something with a blond weave walked past in a spandex outfit that matched his suit, and Mohammed eventually headed in that direction.

I think the person who invented the nightclub had to come from a really dysfunctional family. Think about it. He was sitting around one day, depressed that he wasn't meeting any nice girls, and then he had what he thought was a brilliant idea. "I'll buy some space, play some extremely loud music, serve all kinds of hard liquor, and turn the lights down really low. No wait, I'll turn them off and just have strobe lights. Then I'll let in more people than the maximum limit allowable by the fire department. Yeah, I bet that would be a good way to meet a nice girl."

If anything, trying to meet someone at a club makes you mad that you even have to go out to a place that is more distracting than a naked woman at a monastery.

If I made the rules, first of all, anyone wanting to listen or dance to the music would have to buy headsets, like you do if you want to watch a movie on a plane. That way you could adjust the volume to your liking and you could take them off when you wanted to have a conversation with someone. I would also make sure all clubs were lit up like my grandmother's birthday cake or, even better, like those 99-cent bargain stores. Those stores are so bright, I swear, every time I'm standing in the checkout line I feel like I'm in a police lineup. But that's how bright it should be in clubs because everyone looks good in dim light. You should be able to see *everything*! The bad teeth, bald spots, the cheap shoes.

Women take great pains when going out. I mean sometimes I go through more steps than those scientists have to go through when suiting up to handle killer viruses. From getting our hair laid, to selecting the fiercest outfit in our closet, right down to the small details of the rhinestones on our manicured baby toe. And because clubs are so dark, the only person who notices your miraculous transformation is your girlfriend, who caught a glimpse when the car light was on for a brief moment when you went to pick her up. I mean, why not just get dressed up, turn your music up loud, and go dance in the closet? That way there's no cover charge, and you don't have to worry about someone spilling a drink on you, or about getting the cigarette smoke smell out of your hair and clothes.

I guess we put up with it because, really, we go to clubs hoping to meet a man. And most fellas go there to get lucky, which does not make for an "equal" equation. Of course, some women won't admit that they go to clubs to find a man. "Oh no, girlfriend, I go to clubs to get my groove on." Turn on "Soul Train."

"And I really just go to clubs for the ambiance." Light some candles.

"Girl, I just go to hang out with my girls and have a little drink." Buy a six-pack, go home, and try out your three-way calling.

I'm not saying you can't have fun at clubs. I've gotten into some of my best brawls while clubbing it. Fighting for bathroom mirror space is a killer! And letting a man rub on you while dancing, only to find his woman waiting for you outside, is a picnic. I'm just saying that if you're going to go to a club, you have to look at it for what it is. You shouldn't expect to meet Mr. Right or Mr. Politically Correct, for that matter, in a place that sounds like a trash compactor, is dark, and serves mind-altering drinks. Now, I'm not saying it's impossible to meet someone at a club, because anything is possible. Meeting some-one is never the problem, it's trying to figure out exactly what you've met and agreed to go out with the next day when you return to a state of coherence. I say when you go just be wary and change your expectations and your attitude.

If you do meet someone who, from what you can tell, seems like someone you would like to see again, in a different atmosphere, then by all means go for yours. Tell him your real name, even give him your real number in exchange for his. And the next day, once the buzz dies down, your ears quit ringing, and your pupils are no longer dilated, call the number he gave you. If a woman (his wife, or his mother) doesn't answer, it isn't disconnected (he ain't got a job), and it's not a 1-900 number (he works for the psychic hotline), you might be on to something.

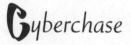yberchase

I recently bought a computer so I could meet men. Seriously, one of my friends told me about how she met a man on the Internet. I had tried every other form of dating, so I figured, why not. After I hooked it up, I immediately enrolled in an online service and went to work.

I navigated my way to a dating chat room where there was some obscure topic being discussed related to 15th-century footwear. I was giving my thoughts, when ALLMAN entered the room and started directing his questions at me. "So, WOOWOO, what's your story?" He took me off-guard, he was so forward. I felt like all cursors were on me. He also made me curious. I wondered what was up with his hard drive. It was obvious he operated on Pentium speed.

I ignored him, but then he sent me a private message asking me to go off to some room where only he and I could talk. Everything in me told me not to go. I don't know what I was thinking. I mean we had only just started interfacing a few minutes ago. I didn't want to get a reputation of being a cyberslut. But against my better judgment, I went in the private room. All of a sudden, my computer screen went a little dim. His words slowly appeared on the screen. They appeared smaller than in the chat room. Apparently he was whispering. Then he started asking me all kinds of personal questions. Like, what was my e-mail address and did I prefer floppys over 3/4 inch. That was enough. I logged off, sprayed my keyboard with disinfectant, and canceled my subscription to my online service. Wasn't that *interneting*?

Let's Get Personal

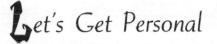 I remember the day I responded to him. It took me over a month because his was like no other I had seen before. It seemed so long and it just went on and on. It was just too good to be true. I knew once I said yes, there would be no turning back. I guess that's why I waited to do it, because I knew it could probably be an uncomfortable and possibly painful experience, especially since I was worried that I wouldn't live up to his expectations. I mean, this was my first time responding to a personal ad.

He turned out to be a really nice guy, but his job ended up transferring him overseas. He begged me to go with him, but quite honestly I wasn't willing to make that move. After all, it was only our second date, and I didn't speak Mandarin.

I have to say, I was skeptical about finding a man the same way you shop for a used car, but at the time, I was having trouble finding a nice boy. There was a drought in my life, both literally and figuratively. You see, it was the summer, I was manless, and everywhere I went I'd see couples. It seemed like God was playing this cruel joke on me. A couple would ride past on a tandem bike. I'd go to a club and couldn't get in because it was "Couples Night Only." I'd sit down to eat my food and see two peas in a pod. It was just ridiculous.

Then my adventurous, will-try-anything-at-least-two-times friend Leslie convinced me to do a Janet Jackson and take "control" of my life. She made me realize that finding a man through the newspaper was not a desperate act. It was simply an efficient, anonymous, fun way to meet people. When I looked at it that way, the thought that I could possibly find my soul mate just by answering an advertisement in the back of a newspaper became kind of intriguing. It was as simple as dating a few hundred strangers who potentially could be psychos, killers, or worse yet, unattractive, and finding the proverbial prize in the Cracker Jack box. How difficult could that be? Then I remembered that sometimes those prizes were stupid and cheap. But I kept on trying.

Cory was my second attempt at finding love through the personal ads. He was new to the dating scene. It probably had something to do with the fact that he was twelve. I should have gotten the hint when he said he wanted to meet at Rat Fun House. But as my friend reminded me, you have to keep an open mind in these situations, so I went along, thinking it was cute. It took me two weeks to calm my nerves from all those hyperactive brats running around like they had lost their minds.

Those kids beat the hell out of that poor rat until he coughed up some more of those stupid tokens so they could buy those worthless toys.

After I got over the shock that the boy was barely half my age, I decided to make the most of the evening. He was an interesting kid. His favorite subject was math. He'd turned over Nintendo twice (whatever that meant). He hadn't wet the bed in two months and he wanted to be an astronaut when he grew up. His parents, who had tagged along, were even more interesting. It turned out that Cory decided to put in a personal ad because he said his parents didn't understand him. His parents decided to take the advice of their therapist and go along with little Cory's request to become independent. Suffice it to say, the date ended early. His curfew was 8 p.m. The evening wasn't a total loss. I actually learned a valuable and simple lesson: Avoid personal ads that are written in crayon.

That experience taught me to pay closer attention to what men wrote in these personal ads. I don't care how he describes himself in his ad, the fact is, we don't see ourselves as others see us. One man's idea of tall, dark and handsome might actually be Herve Villechaize with a tan. "Zee plane, zee plane!" And you forget, sometimes a man might have a different agenda. I mean at first, I would just circle and call all the ads that said single black man. Then it dawned on me that some of them, as I read a little further, would say, "SBM LOOKING FOR SBM," and I realized that I wasn't the one. From there I learned to decipher the codes:

SBM LOOKING FOR ANY RACE WHO LOVES TO TRAVEL = The brother is either very open-minded or he needs your passport to escape the country.

BM LOOKING FOR FRIENDSHIP AND POSSIBLE ROMANCE = Married man who wants to cheat on his wife.

SBM LOOKING FOR GOOD CHRISTIAN-MINDED SBF = He wants a freak of the week.

SBM, WELL READ, WITH ATHLETIC BUILD, LOOKING FOR PEN PAL = He's in prison.

SENSITIVE SBM WITH A FLAIR FOR FASHION, LIKES GOING TO THE THEATER, HAS A LOVE FOR COOKING AND PLANTS, SEEKING SBF FOR CASUAL OR LONG-TERM RELATIONSHIP = He's gay, but he's in denial.

SBM LOOKING FOR SUCCESSFUL BF WHO LIKES NICE THINGS AND ENJOYS THE GOOD LIFE = He's either a gigolo or he plans to rob you.

SWM FROM ABROAD LOOKING FOR EXCITING, CASUAL RELATIONSHIP WITH INDEPENDENT BF WHO LOVES CARS AND LOOKING FOR A GOOD TIME = Hugh Grant.

Pick-Up Lines that Let a Man Know You Are Selectively Single

So maybe the problem for some of us is not where to meet men; maybe it's trying to figure out what to say once you see them. We all have stories of the one who got away. We see him at the health-food store, the gas station, in his car at a stoplight, at the bank, and for some reason we lose our minds and our tongues because all we can think of is—"Hi." As if that's going to make the man say, "Hi, by the way, I'm single and available. Would you like to go out?" That would make things a lot simpler, but unfortunately anything that is worth having you have to work for.

First and foremost, eye contact and a smile are the two most important things you need to make an initial connection with a person. Walking past some man with your head bowed won't get you anywhere. After all, this ain't Japan. And if you're sporting a look on your face that says, "Life's a bitch and then you die," even a man who just needs some spare change isn't going to want to go near you. He probably still will, but believe me he won't feel good about it. A smile says I'm happy, I'm enjoying life, I tithe, I'm in good mental and physical health, and I visit my dentist regularly.

So the next time you see a fine man coming your way, and you only have a few seconds to think of something creative and ingenious to say to let him know you're interested and to find out if he's interested, just memorize these pick-up lines and work it, girl! First, give him the stare and whatever you do, don't take your eyes off of him. Then say as innocently as possible:

"Excuse me for staring, but you look so familiar to me—would your name happen to be Denzel Washington?"

OR

"My doctor wrote me a prescription that requires me to take a caramel-colored brother with a wonderful smile out to dinner. Would you care to fill my prescription?"

OR

"My name is Simpson and I hope your name is Ashford because I'm sure our love would be solid as a rock."

If you're in the produce section you might say:
"Excuse me, I'm making a Josephine Baker costume. Can you tell me which of these bananas would look good on me?"

If you see a man you're attracted to at the ice- or roller-skating rink, skate next to him and fall on purpose so that he'll have to catch you. As he's holding you and looking down into your eyes say innocently:
"I can't believe how easily I fell for you."

Or for you sisters who are looking for a freak, if you see a man in the gym, ask him:
"Would you like to be my trainer? I need someone who doesn't mind using a whip."

OK, what if you're driving down the highway and you look over and see the man of your dreams drive past? What do you do to get his attention? You speed up and hit his bumper—hopefully causing a small fender bender so that he has to stop so you can exchange information. He may initially be upset, but if you say in your sexiest and most demure voice, "There ain't nothing wrong with a little bump and grind is there?" *believe me*, he'll forget all about his fender.

Whether you agree to go out with a guy you meet at a club, or on a blind date, or at the supermarket, chances are you'll know by the middle of the date if it's like going to a Mike Tyson fight only to discover he's fighting Jimmy Walker: It's not a good match, but what can you do? Well, actually there is something you can do if Mr. Suavebolla turns out to be Mr. Thunderbird and you don't want to hurt his feelings. Here are a few suggestions on ways to cut short the date without drawing any suspicion:

✗ "Excuse me, may I use your phone? I need to let the warden know I'm going to be out late tonight."

✗ "I can't remember the last time I used any protection."

✗ "I think personal hygiene is overrated."

✗ "Would you like to buy a *Watchtower*?"

✗ "I'll be right back; I have to change my tampon."

✗ "I've got a long day ahead of me tomorrow. I'm having a vasectomy."

✗ "An exciting new episode of 'Hangin' with Mr. Cooper' is coming on tonight, and I forgot to set my VCR."

✗ "I'll have the lobster."

"I'll have the Cristal."

"I'll have the Chateaubriand."

(NOTE: These can be used individually or all together for more efficiency.)

✗ "My goals? I want to get married and have seven kids."

You Make the Call

Daniel was the perfect blind date, if there is such a thing. My friend Amanda the Matchmaker thought we would make a great couple, so we met at a nice little cafe in Santa Monica.

"Hi, Kim?" I heard a sultry voice say from behind me. When I turned around, I thought I would faint right there on the spot. The man was gorgeous. Not pretty-boy gorgeous, just a rugged, masculine man's man kind of gorgeous. It took

me a full minute to recover from my state of shock and then
he handed me a bouquet of flowers and kissed me on the
cheek.

"Thank you for meeting me."

"No, thank *you*," I said, hoping I would be able to control
the drool that I could feel building on my bottom lip. The
maître d' showed us to our table, and after having a great meal
and good conversation, my date settled the bill and asked if I
would like to take a stroll on the pier. I obliged because I truly
did not want the night to end.

"Kim, I'm really glad we did this. You are really fun to be
with."

"You are too, Daniel." Oh God, I had so many personal
questions. I couldn't believe this man, as fine and as smart as
he was, was still available.

"You have very beautiful eyes."

"Thank you. Daniel, can I ask you a personal question?"

"Sure."

"Are you—is there—do you have—are you in a relationship with someone?" That came out pretty smoothly.

"No. I wouldn't be here if that was the case. That's not
my style. To tell you the truth, Kim, I'm really very shy and my
work keeps me pretty busy. And I guess honestly, I haven't
met the right woman."

"Well, do you think I might be the right woman?" I wanted
to ask. Instead I said, "Yeah, I know, I feel the exact same
way." Suddenly, with the moonlight beaming across my face,
he leaned closer to me and brushed his lips against my cheek.
Then he kissed me on the mouth, ever so gently. We walked
back to our cars, we kissed again, and then he said, "I really
had a nice time. Would it be okay for me to call you tomorrow
and maybe we can get together?"

"Yes, I would like that." He opened my car door and waved to me as I drove away. Thank God for seatbelts. Because I could have done a cartwheel right then and there! No pressure. Good conversation. No expectations. Excellent tongue action. A perfect date.

I woke up early the next morning with a grin on my face and with the energy of a thousand small children who had eaten all the candy in their Easter baskets. First, I opened the windows and breathed the fresh morning air. A dove landed on my arm as I stroked it and fed it some bird seed. After doing an hour on the treadmill, I put in my Donna Richardson video and did another hour of step aerobics. I gave myself a facial, shaved my legs, and arched my eyebrows all before 9:00 a.m. It was Saturday, and I had decided to skip my routine of grocery shopping. I also canceled my breakfast date with a girlfriend because honestly I wanted to be available just in case Daniel wanted to do breakfast—after all, it is the most important meal of the day. I'd also canceled my noon dentist appointment, and my 2 o'clock nail appointment. Besides, there was so much to do around the house.

At 3 o'clock I was on the phone with my girlfriend, asking her to call me back to see if my phone was working. It was. Then I began to panic. What if Daniel was a victim of a U.F.O. abduction? It happens all the time. By 4 o'clock I rationalized that Daniel had probably gotten tied up with work. He did say that they kept him pretty busy. With each passing hour, I got angrier and my memory of him became more and more distorted. Five o'clock. I remembered he was kind of effeminate. Six o'clock. He had that annoying tic. Seven o'clock. He was kind of boring. Eight o'clock. Now that I think about it, when he kissed me, I felt like he was giving me liposuction. Nine o'clock. He was a loser.

Now the thought had occurred to me that he could have lost my number. And that just made me angrier. How could he be so cavalier? I don't just give out my number to any Moe, Curly, or Larry. He should have memorized it. He should have tattooed it on his chest.

We've all been there. You ask yourself, Why do men set us up like that? It's like making one of those ice cream sundaes with all the toppings and then letting you just have a lick. Well, instead of trying to understand why or going through all that wondering and unsolved mystery crap, I've decided if a man says he's going to call and he doesn't, after an appropriate amount of time passes, I make the call. What's an appropriate amount of time? When you feel like it. Okay, so maybe at least wait until he can get home from the date. But hey, if you want to call him that night to say you had a good time, do it. What do you have to lose? Your self-respect? Your pride? I had lost those a long time ago. Besides, that kind of stuff isn't important when it comes to matters of the heart. You can't see those things over a telephone wire anyway.

So at 9:30, I decided to call this man and give him a piece of my mind. I nervously dialed the number. His answering machine picked up. "Hi, Daniel, this is Kim, remember me? Obviously not because you haven't called me. Anyway, I just wanted to say that I think you are the scum of the earth. I see why you don't have anyone special in your life, if you don't even have the courtesy to call someone when you say you're going to call. Not that I was waiting around or anything. But if this is what you're about, then I don't want to have anything to do with you. Don't bother calling me back. You have a nice life and—" Before I could finish my diatribe my call waiting beeped. "Hello?" To my surprise, Daniel was on the other line.

"Hi, Kim, it's me, Daniel. Listen, I got tied up here at the office, but if you're up to it, I thought I could pick up some champagne, and maybe come over to your place and we could rent a movie or something. All I need to do is tie up a couple of things here, check my messages at home, and I could be there in twenty minutes."

"Daniel, hold on a second." I clicked over to the other line where his answering machine was waiting and quickly said, "Gotcha! I was just teasing. Talk to you later." Then I clicked back over to Daniel. "Twenty minutes? That sounds great— oh, and Daniel, you seem like a man with a healthy sense of humor. Am I right?"

The Dating Pain

When I start dating someone I really like, I lose my mind. It's true. It's like the first week at a new job. I dress to impress, I'm efficient, and I'm very accommodating. I want him to like me as much as I like him, and darn it, I want it to last. I think women, in general, feel that way. You ask yourself when would be the right time to tell him your nickname in college was "Mattress Back" or that the two little boys that live with you and have an uncanny resemblance to you aren't really your brothers. If you reveal certain things too soon, a person might be liable to turn you in to the cops to get the reward money. If you wait too long, he might find out what you should have told him up front from a guy named Skippy who lives up the street.

I won't lie; personally I am an open book. Sometimes I can be painfully honest. In the past, I felt that honesty helped to eliminate all the pretense. Since then, I've learned that being honest can also work against you. For example, a guy asked me once, "So, Kim, are you a party animal?"

"Well, if you count the one time I got drunk at a party, stripped naked, and drew happy faces on my nipples, then I guess so." I shouldn't have been surprised when he suggested buying a keg and going back to his place.

Or like when I dated this guy who had a two-year-old son. He asked me one day if his son looked like him because everyone told him the boy looked like his mother. I blurted out, "Does his mother look like E.T.?" Now, while that did eliminate the pretense, it also eliminated any chance of me ever hooking up with him again. So it's hard to figure out what to reveal to a person and when.

And when is it okay to do the tongue dance? Should you at least wait until the first date or does doing it while you're setting up the first date help to get it out of the way? And when does dating turn into a relationship? Is it when he starts keeping his toothbrush and a set of clean drawers at your place on a regular basis? Or is dating and being in a relationship an oxymoron? Or am I a moron just for thinking about this stuff so deeply?

I think these are legitimate questions (except for the one about me being a moron), ones that I believe I have the answers to! You'll find them on the following pages. Finally, a realistic guide to let women know if their hearts are speaking louder than their actions. No longer will you have to ask yourself if you should reconsider letting the man you met two weeks ago move in, especially since you still live with your mother. Check out the guide. And it might do you well to cut it out, shrink it down, laminate it, and refer to it like you do those tip guides when you're at a restaurant. Or you could just read it, get a good laugh, and then commit the tips to memory.

Kim's Guide to the First Date ♥

Kissing ♥ OK	I have never been opposed to kissing on a first date. Kissing is fun and it can tell you a lot about a man: If he's aggressive, if he's sloppy, if he "sucks." And while kissing is a very personal and intimate act and shouldn't be done indiscriminately, sometimes getting it out of the way on the first date can relieve some of the pressure for you both. That doesn't mean you should feel obligated to kiss a man on the first or second or any date for that matter. If you like him and he's got his eyes closed, why not? Just remember where it can lead to and ask yourself if you are prepared to go there.
Going Back to His Place ♥ IT DEPENDS	If we lived in a different time and in a different place, my answer would probably be in the affirmative. But unfortunately, there are a lot of cuckoos for Cocoa Puffs out there. If this is someone you are meeting for the first time and you haven't had the time to have your girlfriend Peaches who works at the DMV do a background check on homeboy yet, I wouldn't be too quick to run back to his place for a night- or day-cap, for that matter. If it's a friend of Rae Rae's from around the way who knows he's good people, then going back to his place is probably okay. Just remember where it could lead to and ask yourself if you are prepared to go there!

Paying for the Meal

♥

IT DEPENDS

While some brothers may get offended if you reach into your purse and pull out cash instead of a Tic Tac after a meal, a real man will be flattered. Be sincere, don't do it just because you're looking for him to say, "Don't worry, baby, I got this." 'Cuz he just might call your hand. If you asked him out, you should definitely bring your checkbook, but if it's the other way around, then he should pay. If you're feeling overly generous and he asked you out, you can still offer to pay. Formalities shouldn't rule your heart, but be careful about setting a precedent.

Buying Him a Gift

♥

IT DEPENDS

Okay, if you've already paid for dinner and now you're handing him a present, he might feel like a gigolo. When we really think we're going to like someone, we tend to have a generous spirit, but it's better to wait awhile until you at least know if he even prefers boxers over briefs before blowing the cash. Now if his birthday happens to be on the day of your first date, giving him a present would be thoughtful. Just keep it simple. If you're checking out the Rolex counter, that's not my idea of simple!

Having Sex

♥

NOT OK

All I have to say is one word. AIDS. Okay maybe I have more than one word: HIV. Okay maybe three words: HERPES COMPLEX XIV, or SY-PHI-LIS. If life holds any value for you, 15 minutes of passion with someone you know very little about could be a death sentence. We all want to sample the merchandise, but in this case, the defective merchandise cannot be returned to the store. Get tested, get to know each other, *get a condom*. And if your libido gets the best of you, remember where it could lead and ask yourself if you are prepared to go there! R.I.P.

Saying "I love you"

♥

NOT OK

It may be love at first sight, but I wouldn't be inclined to tell a man that on the first date. Besides him thinking you're not playing with a full deck, he might just say "I love you" back. Then it would be official that both of you weren't dealing in reality. Unless you're using that term loosely, I would save that for a later date, like after you've gotten to know him better. Take your time.

Telling Him You're a Virgin

♥

IT DEPENDS

If you find yourself in a compromising situation and you want out, telling him you're a virgin might help, even if you're not. However, if you're at dinner and he's asking you to tell him something about yourself, while I would be quite proud of being a virgin, I'm not sure I would reveal that on the first date. Besides him not believing you, it'll throw his concentration off. You should probably wait until he asks, or at least save it until you're in a private place, where people can't hear him cracking up because he thinks you're joking, or see him drool over the thought of navigating your uncharted territory.

Passing Gas

♥

IT DEPENDS

Let's face it. Sometimes when you got to go, you got to go. Holding something like that in could kill you. Generally, though, you want to wait awhile before you decide to lay something that heavy past him. Preferably after he's told you he loves you. If he loves you, it might smell a little sweeter to him. (I doubt it.) In any case, if it's the first date and you break wind, be prepared for him to set sail and say, "See ya!"

Telling Him You Have Eleven Kids

♥

IT DEPENDS

If you want him to stick around for a second date, you should know that revealing that you have more children than his dog's litter will more than likely scare him away. Although it may be kind of difficult to hide if you tell him he needs to change the dinner reservation to 13 and you're going to need three high chairs because your babysitter backed out. Then again, he may be forming a baseball team so it might be good for him to know. In all fairness, when you have children, and they aren't hidden away in the attic, it's best to let the guy know up front. It should be his prerogative if he wants to deal. Likewise, he should let you know right away if he's fathered a small country.

Revealing Your Family Medical History

♥

IT DEPENDS

I don't think it's any of his business to know right away that you spend most of your holidays at a mental institution visiting your relatives. If you've inherited the insanity gene, believe me, he should be able to tell without you mentioning it. However, if you have multiple personalities, you might want to tell him on the first date just in case he decides he likes the one that goes by the name of Sybil more than you.

Introducing Your Parents

♥

NOT OK

If your parents are anything like mine, you might want to wait until after he says, "I do." Just teasing. Unless your parents happen to be at the same restaurant, bowling alley, etc. (and even then I would try to avoid them) I would say get a rain check. Parents have a way of making an uncomfortable situation more uncomfortable. "So Kimmy tells me you're a doctor." "No ma'am, I'm not." "I can dream can't I?" Or "Would you like to see a picture of my Kimmy before dental work was done? Oh, and here is a picture of her without the weave." Gently ease him into meeting "the folks" and make sure your mother looks good, because if she is aging badly, he'll run away so he doesn't have to be around to see *you* get old.

Moving in Together

♥

NOT OK

Unless your roommate ran out on you and your landlady is threatening to have a garage sale with your things to cover your roommate's part of the rent, I say remain solo for a while. Besides, if you're thinking about marrying this man down the line, if you move in with him, he just might change his mind. You might change yours, for that matter. If you're lonely, get a fish. If you find he spends most of his time at your place anyway, kick him out some nights. You both need room to breathe sometimes.

Getting Married

♥

HELL NO!

Next to chastity, marriage is the most serious vow you will make in your lifetime. Okay, maybe chastity is a vow only a few of us will make. The point is, marriage is something that shouldn't be rushed into. Yeah, it's okay to fantasize or try his last name on for size on the first date. It's even okay to wonder about what your children will look like. For example, a first date with Shaquille O'Neal would have me doing this: Mrs. Kimberley O'Neal, or "Kim & Shaq cordially invite you to their housewarming on the tenth." "Shaq, darling, it's a boy!" But just throwing caution and your mind, for that matter, to the wind and marrying a man you just met could only mean two things. You're a serious risk-taker and feel you have nothing to lose, or you're being deported in the morning and there's no way around it. Good luck!

Do the Bright Thing

There was a time when I was adamantly opposed to it. I mean, it seemed everyone was doing it because it was the "in" thing. Because you did it out in the open, exposing yourself, it made you look cool. Then we learned it had long-term effects on your skin. Sun bathing, silly. I guess I was against interracial dating too. My thinking was, just because Oreo cookies got it going on didn't mean that blacks and whites should hook up. I felt we must preserve our culture and pass on to our children a heritage and history of African ancestry that they can both be proud and honored to be a part of. You know, keep up the strong Mandigo warrior bloodline.

Whenever I see a mixed couple I have very opposite, very immediate, very strong, well, mixed emotions. On one hand I start humming "We Are the World" and I think about how wonderful it is that they have overcome this society's silly notions of race and all that us vs. them crap. I think about how brave they are and wish the best for the couple and their beautiful beige babies. And then I wonder how they ever got together in the first place. Are they denying their own race and culture to favor the other? Are they trying to forget which team they are on? I start humming that song that Maria's cousin (Rita Moreno) in West Side Story sings, "Stick to Your Own Kind," and contemplate their confused beige babies.

Speaking of children, I'll admit that some combinations of certain races do make pretty kids. Black mixed with anything comes out nice! I think black and Asian is gorgeous, white and Asian is lovely, and any Latino concoction comes out nicely too. True story—I once dated a man who was 1/4 East Indian, 1/4 black, 1/4 Native American, 1/4 Irish. And as if that wasn't complicated enough, he had been adopted by Jewish parents. I promise I am not making this up. First question I wanted to ask was how the hell did all them people hook up to make him? Second question was what type of food did he grow up eating? Probably curried vegetarian spicy ribs with maize, washed down with beer eaten while wearing a yarmulke. Huh? And we thought that Rae Dawn Chong had it hard. He was beautiful; a little confused, but beautiful. Oh sure, he got to celebrate *all* the holidays, but he didn't know if he should pray to Jesus or Buddah or Mohammed, or do a rain dance when he needed guidance. I had to stop dating him. I got scared that our children might come out plaid!

Now the interracial dating issue is a hot topic for black women. You want to see a mad sistah? Show me a handsome black man with his arm around a white woman and *Pow*— instant angry black woman! For all she knows the brother could be helping someone who tripped and fell (yeah right), but she sees black, then white, then RED!

I think we get so upset because first of all there really is a shortage of good available brothers. I read somewhere that there was something like nine eligible white men for every ten white women. But our statistics are a little grim: seven of our men are available for every ten of us. They are in jail, they are gay, there are simply less of them because more women are born in the world. Add to that the high mortality rate for young black men—especially in urban areas—and you can understand why a single black woman has less of a pool to chose from. And we want to swim. Look at me trying to kick some knowledge.

When I see the brothers with white women, I want to ask what, why, and how. What have we done to turn you away? Why do you not want us anymore? How can we get back in your good graces? I assume that when a black man turns away from the sistahs, he has rejected us and no longer finds us desirable and beautiful. Boo-hoo.

Part of the problem is that this country uses Caucasian standards for judging beauty (just look at any magazine rack). All of this is beginning to change, though, because America's "face" is changing. There is much more ethnic diversity. Some brothers got brainwashed into believing that long silky hair, fair skin, and sharp features are better than our kinky curly hair, brown skin, and rounded features. And our brothers fall for that hype faster than it took Robert Shapiro to diss Johnny Cochran after the first O.J. trial. I think there is room for all types of beauty (except if you look like a hump-backed bearded gargoyle, and even they need somebody to love!).

Just like a lot of sistahs, I want to know what compels our men to go from behind the wheel to the back seat with Miss Daisy. I mean really, what does Anna Nicole Smith have that I don't? Poor example. Ask a brother and you normally get the same pat answer: "She treats me special. She doesn't hassle me, and she's beautiful." Translation: "She's passive and although you do have a better ass you are too damn demanding!"

Well, for all the men out there who don't want us anymore, let me remind you of a few things. Look at who they got and look at who we got. They got: Betsy Ross. We got: Sojourner Truth. They got: Kate Moss. We got: Tyra Banks. They got: Jenny Jones. We got: Oprah. They got: Meryl Streep. We got: Angela Bassett. They got: Reba, The Judds, and Cyndi Lauper. We got: Whitney, Salt 'N Pepa, and Queen Latifah. They got: Paula Abdul and Mariah Carey. We got: them too, they really are black despite what you read in the magazines. They got: Hazel. We got: Florence from "The Jeffersons." They got: Susan Lucci. We got: Susan Lucci. Oh please, black folks love themselves some Erica Kane. They got: Paula Poundstone. We got: Kim Coles. Huh? We got it going on, too! Just ask Roger Ebert, Robert DeNiro, and Hugh Grant. They have all been "turned on to the dark side"!

There have been three incidents in my life that have opened my vistas about interracial dating. The first was that my brother married someone white. I adore her because she adores my brother. They have a wonderful bond that goes beyond any stereotypes, taboos, experiments, or rules. They simply love one another, and it doesn't hurt that I think my brother is well endowed. (I used to change his diapers.) And at present they are expecting a little beige baby. The second incident was a conversation with one of my dearest, most trusted black male friends, who said to me once, "I love the black woman, but if I happened to meet a woman who was kind and sweet and intelligent who could love me and was right for me and she just happened to come in a white package, would you deny me that wonderful experience?" And I told him I wouldn't, because it really seemed to come from a pure place. The third incident was the most eye-opening. I cannot say that I have never seen an interesting white guy; come on, a cute guy is a cute guy. I do prefer chocolate, but I admit that one day I met a vanilla who was a terrific guy. We became friends because we had a lot in common. Against my better judgment, I started to develop feelings for him, and—although I never did act on them because I was embarrassed, and I really want to hold out for a brother—I later became proud that I was able to overlook his race to see the good person inside. There has never been a kiss, never any nookie, but what we share in our friendship is deeper than some intimate relationships I've had. And I cherish that.

The Denzel Factor

The result of research I've done on the number-one reason why black couples end a relationship will astound you, or perhaps it won't because it has probably happened to some of you: The Denzel Factor.

We cannot deny the man is not only fine, he's smart, he's mysterious, and he has a black wife—kudos! And just in case things don't work out, we all secretly want to be the next Mrs. Washington. We know this, and believe me, our men know it too. That is why it is important that while you are in a relationship, if possible, avoid the mention of this man's name. I repeat, do not mention Denzel Washington's name in the company of your significant other. It will set even the most secure man off like a rocket! DENZEL WASHINGTON MOVIES ARE STRICTLY FOR GIRLFRIEND OUTINGS! Avoid going with your significant other to a movie that stars Denzel Washington. You may want to go so far as checking to make sure that the previews do not feature Denzel. (And just to be on the safe side, you might want to rip these pages out of the book, just so he won't know you've been reading about Denzel.) I speak from experience, ladies.

My *in*significant other and I mistakenly went to see *The Preacher's Wife*. Don't ask me why, but for some reason I dressed extra special for the movie, even put on some new perfume. Five minutes into the movie, my *in*significant other decided he wanted to get all amorous. Never before in the history of our relationship had he ever tried to grab my breast in a movie theater in an effort to be romantic. Never before had he tried to ram his tongue down my throat while watching a movie in a movie theater. The Denzel Factor, ladies. He sensed the power of Denzel and his ego took over.

Denzel is not the first one to have this power to make black women, and men for that matter, lose their minds. I suspect Billy Dee Williams is the reason why my parents are divorced today. So remember ladies, if you go with your man to see Denzel in a movie, be afraid, be very afraid.

Dateless and Not Doing a Damn Thing About It

So many rules! It's no wonder many of us opt to pass on the dating scene and instead elect to get to know the video store personnel on a first name basis. Staying home, renting videos, complaining to your girlfriend that you're lonely, is safe. While you might not know the ending of the movie, you know that the evening is going to end without you having to take a risk.

There was a time when my girlfriend Tracy and I, because we were such homebodies, would always talk during the week about going out on the weekend to better our chances of meeting men.

"Hey, girl, I understand Sinbad's HBO premiere party is on Saturday. We should go."

"That sounds good. Oh, and I heard the Big Brothers organization is having a Singles Only night down at the Pavilion. It might be fun."

And lo and behold the weekend creeps up on us and we'd make excuses:

"I don't have anything to wear."

"Isn't that place pretty far?"

"My hair is a mess."

"I think my goldfish has the flu."

"You want to just order a pizza and rent some videos?"

Well, I've got news for you, you're not going to find someone by sitting at home wondering when you're going to find someone. It doesn't work that way. Unless you're under house arrest, there is no reason why you should be sitting at home alone on a weekend unless you want it that way. Take a chance. Maybe you've just had a break-up or you're going through a divorce and you're not ready to get back out there. That's understandable, take some time. But sometimes just getting out of the house to get some fresh air might be what you need. When you think you might be ready to date again, get out there and meet some nice people and have some fun. Oh, and don't forget to take along your dating guide; it might come in handy!

♥

You Don't Hear Me, Though

met Darnell in a bar in Queens when I was very young, very naive, and thirsty for some Champale. What can I say; I was young. What impressed me most about him was his quick wit and his penchant for nice things . . . gold chains, gold teeth, gold hubcaps. What can I say; I was young. He said he was a pharmaceutical salesman, a fact that I knew would please my mother a great deal. My first professional man! Our whirlwind courtship lasted two weeks before things started to turn into the dating twilight zone. He called me early one morning to let me know that he had been arrested. It turned out that Darnell was really a small-time drug dealer (which would explain why those pills he gave me for my P.M.S. made me feel *really* happy). What can I say; I was young. He got busted, plea bargained, and received a 14-month sentence. I was devastated, but because I was "in love," I forgave his deception, and vowed to see him through the whole terrible ordeal.

Thanks to watching the movies *Penitentiary I, II,* and *III,* I had a pretty good idea of the kind of suffering he would endure in the Big House. To compensate for what I could only imagine was a horrible experience, I would send him care packages with love poems, inspirational messages like "even the caged bird sings," and pictures of myself, hoping to lift his spirits. He called me one day to tell me how he was feeling.

"I can't take it no more, Kim. I miss you so much."

"I miss you, too."

"I'm gonna bust if we can't be together soon."

"You only have four hundred and five more days to go."

"Kim, look here, I need to see you. I need you, baby."

"I need you, too."

"Why don't you come up next weekend."

"Okay."

"And wear that dress I like so much."

So it was set. The next weekend I made the trek to the state prison in the dress that Darnell liked so much. I thought against wearing it because I personally thought it was inappropriate for a jail setting. It was way too revealing, and way too short, but then I thought about the joy it would bring to Darnell when he saw me in it. I decided it would probably be one of the highlights of our visit.

While waiting for what seemed like an eternity, I began to daydream about our reunion. The tears in our eyes, the glass partition obstructing our ability to touch. I envisioned us dramatically putting our hands to the glass, remembering a much happier time. And then, finally, after pressing our palms against the partition in an effort to feel closer to one another, we would both breathe a sigh of frustration. I thought about how difficult it would be to look him in the eyes. Not because of his deceit, but because the condensation that built up on the glass would cloud our view. We would then reluctantly pick up the phones and cry silently into the mouthpiece, whispering little nothings. The guard would be so touched, he would give us extra time together. What can I say; I was young, and had an active imagination.

My fantasy was dashed, however, when a guard brusquely escorted me, along with the other visitors, to a huge room filled with open tables.

We were instructed to sit individually at the tables and after another thirty minutes, Darnell and the other prisoners appeared from behind a locked door. He took his place across from me. I could tell he was very happy to see me.

"Girl, you look so good. Even better than them pictures you sent me."

"Oh, Darnell, you don't look so bad yourself. Orange isn't your color, though. Those jumpers don't come in brown?"

"Actually, I've had a conversion since the last time we spoke. It's Fuqua Kashir Kumee now."

"I've never heard of that color. It looks orange to me . . . oh, oh, you're a Muslim. Well, ah salim walick up. Whatever."

"Look here, baby, I've been waiting for this for a long time. I've been dreaming about it. Now come over here," he said as he patted his lap, like I was supposed to come running like a golden retriever.

"Is that allowed?" I said, still thinking about that glass partition thingee.

"Come over here." The next thing I knew I was on Darnell's lap and he began kissing me. Then all of a sudden, he started groping me like he was kneading dough. I jumped up in a panic.

"Darnell, I've heard of public displays of affection, but come on! There's other peo—" No sooner had I gotten the words out when, out of the corner of my eye, I saw a couple to my left engaging in the same behavior. In fact, as I turned my attention to the whole room, every woman there, to my horror, was involved in some type of horseback-riding maneuver.

"What's wrong?" he asked, apparently confounded by my reaction.

I couldn't even look him in the face. I signaled for a guard and told Darnell I never wanted to see him again. I cried all the way home, as I tried to figure out what I could have possibly said to make him think that I would actually give him "some" in a room full of people, in a *prison*. Is that what they mean by group sex? I mean, I've heard of sex on the beach, even sex in an elevator, but sex in a room full of *hard* criminals . . . okay, maybe it makes sense looking at it that way. The point is somewhere along the line there was a serious breakdown in the way we communicated.

No doubt, communication is one of the most important skills that has to be mastered if we want to have successful relationships. Oftentimes, it's also the most difficult. My last boyfriend had voice mail, a pager, a cellular phone, a satellite dish, and a car phone, and we still couldn't communicate.

What do we expect, when we couldn't even really communicate as children? Remember how we responded when we liked each other as little boys and girls? Remember how you acted when you were a five-year-old kid and you started having those strange feelings, that you'd never felt before, for little

Stevie? You had this incredible urge to go upside his head with a baseball bat. That was your way of expressing how you felt. Or maybe he tugged at your pig tails or tried to bite the living shit out of you. That was his way of saying he liked you. And let's not forget blowing those nasty, wet spit balls at each other. The wetter the spit ball, the more he liked you. At five years old we're not sophisticated enough to understand those feelings, so hitting and biting seem quite natural. Then once we learn how to read and write, the aggressive behavior subsides, and we start passing notes. You remember those eloquent, well-crafted notes, don't you?

Will You Go With Me?

Please check one:

☐ **YES**

☐ **MAYBE**

☐ **NO**

To our amazement, that form of communication actually worked. It was efficient, straightforward, and you had it in writing just in case he said yes, and then changed his mind later. By our teen years, with those raging hormones beginning to surface, we learned that if he rubbed you on your thigh, you knew he was crazy about you. If you gave him some smooches, or a hickey or monkey bite (as they were called depending on where you grew up), enough said.

As adults, we graduate to actually verbalizing how we feel. Often, you end up hurting his feelings by saying something you didn't mean in the heat of an argument. Or perhaps you did mean it, but you never wanted him to know how you really felt. Like, "Your brother is a better lover than you, anyway." Or he suggests that maybe you should start visiting the gym again. So just like children, we hurt each other, now with words, when we are trying to let the opposite sex know how we feel.

It's amazing how in the first three months of a relationship there are very few communication problems. Think about it. You both have similar agendas. You want him to like you. He wants to get in your panties. So you're both on your best behavior for those first three months. He listens more intently when you talk. You ask safe questions like "What are your hobbies?" or "What kind of cheese do you like?" Because you have the blinders on, he can do no wrong, no matter what he says or does. But after that new car smell goes away, and when he starts to do something that bothers you, it becomes kind of difficult to say "When you spank me during sex, could you not use so much sting?" Or he feels too awkward to tell you "Baby, I don't think it was necessary for you to page me, I just went to the bathroom."

So in the beginning, once we accomplish the task at hand, we hold back our true feelings and lie so as not to hurt each other. That's not to say that's a bad thing—all of the time. I mean, wouldn't you much rather hear "Look at it this way, at least with two stomachs they'll never get lonely" than "Your belly's so big that when your stomach growls, I run and get my earthquake kit." It's understandable that you wouldn't want to communicate how you're really feeling in a situation like that.

There are certain things we say to each other when we're in relationships that you know right from jump are lies. See if you can relate.

Lie Detectors

MEN

"I called, but your machine wasn't on."

You know he's lying because your answering machine is always on. It's called voice mail, fellas. Most women will understand if you're too tired or just want to be by yourself, even though the two of you made plans. Why make her feel like she's paranoid? Stop tripping and own up to the fact that you didn't feel like being bothered.

"We don't have to do nothing. I just want to hold you."

Show me a man who says that and means it, and I'll show you a mountain lion who's a vegetarian. Men say that so we will let down our guard. The next thing you know, your legs are up in the air, and he's snaking you like you're a clogged drain.

I admire a man more if he says, "I just want to do you, and then go home." He still won't have anything coming his way, except my respect and appreciation for his honesty, but that has got to be worth something.

"I promise not to come in your mouth."

When a man is being siphoned, he's liable to say anything to make it a more pleasurable experience for him. Don't believe the hype. Men think a "head" when it comes to such delicate details. They don't want there to be a wet spot to sleep in if they can help it.

"Yeah, I see you in my future."

Just how far in the future, is what you really want to know. Unlike most women, I think most men like to take relationships one day at a time. Or in some cases, one hour at a time. If they go beyond that, somehow they think they have to go out and book a church. If talking about the future makes you uncomfortable, then say so.

"Of course I love you."

If a man doesn't volunteer this information, and you're staring at him like a cocker spaniel about to be put to sleep, then of course he might offer that verbiage out of obligation. Let a man bring his offerings to you in his own time, that way you won't have to wonder if he just said it because you put him on the spot.

WOMEN

"I'm not mad."

Sistah friends, you know you're mad as hell and don't want to take it anymore. That vein pulsating in your forehead and that vise grip you got around his neck give it away every time. I say let the anger out now because you know women have memories like elephants. We'll remember something he did wrong and will wait eight months to scold him. Deal with those feelings while they're fresh in your mind, so you won't have to revisit the matter the next time he mucks up.

"It's not you, I'm just a little confused."

Men will fall for the sympathy act most of the time. Besides, many of them have fragile egos, and if they suspect it's something they've done, they'll be devastated for life, or at least until the next woman comes along and tells them, "It's not you . . . It's me."

Even though it's uncomfortable, if there is something he's doing that's turning you off, it's best to tell him because he just might be able to correct the problem. That way you won't have to walk around dazed all the time.

"It doesn't matter if I don't come."

Yeah, I just sweated out my freshly done hair for the fun of it. If we are equal partners, women want equal satisfaction. Now I understand the law of averages are on the man's side, but these days women have great expectations too. We need to stop playing the martyr and let Speedy McGreedy know, if at all possible, you'll have what he's having!

"Don't worry, I'm on the pill."

The key question to ask here is, "Yeah, but are you taking those bad boys on a regular basis?" Every third Sunday is *not* a regular basis. If a woman asks you to take her to see *Pocahontas*, has an extensive stuffed animal collection, her main topic of conversation is breastfeeding, and she's pushing thirty, wear your raincoat or you just might be in for eighteen years of some stormy weather.

"I love you."

Women will say this prematurely sometimes just to get a reaction out of a man. She may no more love you than she loves doing her laundry. If she waits a full beat and gives you that puppy dog look after she says it, she's trying to gauge the relationship. Before those words come out of our mouths, sistahs, we should first imagine him destitute and impotent, and then see if we can verbalize the same claim.

Express Yo'self

I am very good at expressing how I feel when I'm in a relationship. If he asks, and even if he doesn't, a man will know almost everything about how I feel on every subject in a matter of weeks. I want him to know up front what he's getting into. Sure, it takes away some of the mystery, the allure, but again, to me it eliminates the pretense and any overblown expectations he might have.

And remember, communication is a two-way street. When you tell someone how you feel, you have to realize that whatever you say will affect that person, and they may not respond the way you want them to.

I remember when I was in a relationship where I felt like I was at the bottom of this brother's "things to do" list. So, I sat him down and told him how I felt. "You know, I just feel like life is this big movie where you're the star, and I'm like this little extra that no one cares about." You know what he told me?

"That's a wrap!" And that was the end of our relationship.

If your birthday is coming up and you're dating a man who has not been through a birthday with you, don't expect him to know to do something extra special. Now, I know what some of you are saying: "I shouldn't have to tell him to do something special for my birthday, he should just automatically know to do it." Well, even an automatic dishwasher has to be turned on.

I have a friend whose boyfriend, during the first year of their courtship, gave her a birthday card. He didn't take it out of the bag. He didn't put her name on the envelope. He didn't even sign it! She didn't accept it. She told him how it made her feel, and she expressed how disappointed she was. He felt really bad. Suffice it to say the next year on her birthday he made up for it big time. He gave her a card—he took it out of the bag. It had her name on it and he had autographed it, "*Signed, Sealed, Delivered . . . I'm Yours.*" And taped to the back of the card was an engagement ring. On bended knee, he proposed and promised to make every one of her birthdays more special than the next. I can't imagine how he could ever top that one. The moral of the story is she was able to express how she felt, and he was able to listen and understand her needs.

"Well, Kim, what do you do when you can't find the words, or what if every time they come out wrong?" you ask. It's true some people can't articulate their feelings very well. I have another friend who, if her man asks her how she feels, she shuts down like an illegal business after a police raid. But I believe we are all entitled to our feelings, and we should express those feelings no matter how difficult it might be. Even if you have to sky-write it out for him. When that's not an option, I feel the best way to let a man know what's going on inside is to sit down and write him a letter. I am a firm believer in this method because that way, you don't have to worry about stumbling over your words, he can't interrupt you, and he can read it over and over again until the point sinks in.

"Well, what do I say?" Don't worry, I got that covered. At last, an all-purpose letter that you can construct to your loved one in five minutes. Check it out. Just insert one of the words or phrases that best describes how you are feeling, and you're all set.

My _____ :

1. *dearest darling*
2. *no good ex-lover*
3. *fellow American*

I feel if I don't get this off of my chest I will

_____ .

1. go insane
2. shoot you and then turn the gun on myself
3. miss the opportunity to give you some valuable news

First of all, let me say how _____

1. kind
2. insensitive
3. civic-minded

you are. How you've gotten through life being so

_____

1. wonderful
2. stupid
3. patriotic

is amazing to me. I thank _____

1. God for you
2. my therapist for giving me the strength to get rid of your ass
3. you for being an upstanding citizen

Remember that time you _____?

1. walked in the pouring rain with me to the store
2. beat me and left me for dead
3. paid that high tax bill last year

Well, what you don't know is _____.

1. I have loved you ever since that moment
2. I'm alive and I'm coming after your ass
3. you won't have to worry about that anymore

So _____

1. I hope you feel the same way
2. watch your back
3. vote for me in November

because _____. I hope you realize that

1. I'm having your baby
2. I mean business
3. there is an election booth near you

_____ . I look forward to_____ .

1. I'm not asking anything
   from you
2. I'm watching your every
   move
3. I'm the woman who
   can turn this country
   around

1. hearing your thoughts
2. whipping that ass
3. getting your vote

With all my _____ .

1. love
2. hatred and venom
3. deepest patriotism

_____

1. (Your name)
2. the one you left for dead
3. Kim Coles for president

The Truth about Bats and Hogs

One reason men and women don't understand each other is because we see things from two different points of view. Some women are like bats: we can't see what's right in front of us to save our lives and, therefore, we hang around longer than we should when the relationship sours. Some men are like hogs, on the other hand, and not only eat you out of house and home, but can be pig-headed when it comes to recognizing the relationship for what it is. If a man isn't interested in having a committed relationship, he is more likely to sit you down and say, "Now, I feel like I need to let you know up front that I'm not ready for a committed relationship." The woman manages to hear everything but the word *not*. And two months later, she's crying because she can't understand why he's seeing other people.

Remember men and women are socialized very differently. Men have that "never let them see you sweat" mentality. Men are taught to keep a tight rein on their emotions because showing their feelings makes them more vulnerable. Therefore, it's hard to tell what they're thinking most of the time. Come to think of it, the only time I know how a man feels is when he's watching a serious game of sports or during sex. The grunts give it away. Otherwise, it's a mystery.

Sex can be like a truth serum for some men. During sex, anything a man says, he really means—for that moment, any way. While making love, I've gotten six marriage proposals, three offers to buy me a fur coat, and twenty-one "I swear I'll never leave you"s. And that was just in one night. Then right after they orgasm, they go back to acting deaf and dumb.

Because half the time women don't know what men are thinking, we tend to over-analyze what they say and do. For instance, my friend called me all excited after her third date with a guy she really liked. "Girl, he asked if he could hold my hand. I think he wants to marry me." Now as a woman, I find that deduction quite logical. Let me break it down. It's a tradition for a man to ask a woman for her hand in marriage. Therefore, by asking to hold my friend's hand, this guy was really, on a very deep subconscious level, asking her to marry him. Hold hand = hand in marriage = marriage proposal. See how that connects? (It's quite obvious, really.) Or when this guy I had been dating for a month, who normally called me once a week, happened to call me twice in one week, I thought, "He loves me."

With women, on the other hand, it's hard *not* to know what we are feeling. I mean, how many men do you know who will shed a tear when Frosty the Snowman melts? No matter how many times I watch that, it gets me every time. And there are just no words to describe how I felt when they took out James Earl Jones in *The Lion King*.

When a woman comes home from work and tells you her boss said something crude, she just wants you to listen and sympathize, even empathize with her. She wants you to be her sounding board. What she does not want is your advice on how to handle the situation the next time. She does not want you to call her supervisor and give him or her a piece of your mind. The best thing you can say is, "Aw, baby, I'm sorry. Is there anything I can do?" Or if she complains to you that she can't stand her best girlfriend 'cuz she's a liar, and then the next day she jumps up and goes to the mall with her, don't question it. That's just her way of venting. Women curse out their girlfriends behind their backs, and then the next day, turn around and go shopping with them.

Music to My Ears

Men aren't crazy when it comes to communicating with women. Some of them learned a long time ago what to say to make a woman respond. Just listen to some of the lyrics that are out there. You have men making claims that sound as good as those pyramid schemes. "I'll love you until the break of dawn. Baby, I'll pay your mortgage, your child support for all your kids, whatever it takes for you to be mine." Is that a fantasy or what?

The first time I heard Babyface's song "Soon as I Get Home," I wondered what kind of woman inspired him to write that. The song is about a man promising to do everything for his woman from preparing her meals to doing all of the shopping, and on top of that, to always tell the truth. I was depressed for two days afterward because I couldn't even get a guy to commit to going to a movie, let alone cooking me dinner. I had a guy croon the same tune to me once, but the title of the song was "Soon as I Get Out of Rehab."

Love songs can be a dangerous thing for women because we listen to them and we begin to buy into it. These fantasy island men do not exist. Don't believe the hype. The sooner you realize this, the faster the pain will go away.

There is a song called "Let Me Be Your Housekeeper, Girl." In the video the guy is picking out his woman's clothes and steaming them, then drawing her bath. Now, as romantic as that is, ladies, you know if some man offers to be your housekeeper, you're not going to waste his talents on ironing. You're going to be trying to get him to clean out that damn refrigerator, take the garbage out, or mow the lawn that hasn't been cut in so long it looks like Jurassic Park.

I think we would all be much better off if men just wrote the songs like they really mean them.

The Bottom Line Is, I Want Your Love Tonight

Baby, I want to get next to you.

Tell me what I need to do.

But let me tell you off the bat.

I ain't got enough money to feed my cat.

Love you all night long?

I can love you for a minute or two, then I'm gone.

Say you want me to buy your clothes?

How about if I suck your toes?

You want me to cook you dinner by candlelight?

I told you my money is real tight.

The bottom line is, I want your love tonight.

This way we can cut straight to the chase.

And it's not just love songs that hinder our communication. It's also the fact that men and women have different ideas about what sexual fantasies should entail. Ask a woman about her sexual fantasies and you get descriptions of sunsets, romantic walks on the beach, soft caresses, Luther Vandross singing in the background, lots of foreplay, and slow, slow lovemaking.

Ask a man to describe his sexual fantasy, and if he's honest, the picture will be a lot different. For starters, his fantasy would include a small village of women—with at least one set of lesbians, crotchless underwear, some 2 Live Crew music and a video (preferably "Pop that Coochie"), some handcuffs, and a baby goat.

Seriously, most women equate sex with love and commitment, and for black women this is even more true because we have to make up for those 400 or so years of being separated from our men. Men, on the other hand, equate sex with—sex. Think about it. Normally when women are longing for a mate, someone to share their hopes and dreams with, we say, "I need a man." Most brothers, meanwhile, when thinking about the opposite sex, will say, "I need some putang!"

Covering the Bases Before Reaching Home Plate

Tell brothers you believe in monogamy, and they think you're talking about that movie with Diana Ross and Billy Dee Williams. The only way we are going to truly bridge the "crap" between the sexes is to start communicating our expectations *before* we have sex. If Mike Tyson would have communicated just a little bit to Desiree Washington what his idea of a normal sexual encounter was *before* it happened, perhaps Mike wouldn't have had to take that three-year vacation. I will admit, Desiree sent mixed messages from the get-go too. To call a brother up at two a.m., and then go to his hotel room in only a tiara and a Ms. Indiana ribbon, you're asking for trouble. And if Clarence Thomas would have thought *before* he opened his nasty mouth, Anita Hill wouldn't have had to go there and embarrass him on national TV. If Rick James would have asked that poor woman whether getting beaten turned her on *before* he started whipping her ass, maybe he wouldn't have done his little retreat from freedom. Although his songs "Give It to Me Baby" and "SuperFreak" should have been clues enough for the woman to stay away from him.

To truly understand each other we must first learn each other's language. It's really quite simple. Once you've mastered the phrases below, we will have a better understanding of each other's needs and wants, and will be better able to deal.

#1   WHAT YOU HEARD: "I LOVE YOU."

What he really said: "I love working it on out with you (throwing down in the bedroom) as long as you don't pressure me about marriage, because it's hard being a black man in this world, and as long as you continue to make me feel like a man."

Really, what does love got to do with it? Love is an emotion that some men change, like they change their drawers, when something don't smell right no more. It's not what he says. It's what he does. My girlfriend had a birthday party and she complained because her man of three years didn't bring—didn't think about bringing—a gift. You know what he said? "You know I love you. I showed up, didn't I? That should tell you something." Yeah, it tells me you're a cheap, selfish bastard, who won't get invited next year! *"Love" is an action word.* If he *says* he loves you and does the wild thang with your friend, he don't love you. If she *says* she loves you and goes clubbing with her girls every night, she don't love you. If he *says* he loves you and after ten years of living together will not marry you, he doesn't love you. Love yourself and find you a new love, because you're just wasting your time.

I know what some of you are thinking: "Well, my man don't cheat," "She don't go out with her girls," and "Hell, we've only been dating for six months, but I still don't know if he loves me." If you want to know if he loves you, ask yourself this question: Have you tried the Love Puff test? That is when you fart under the covers in bed, let it marinate for 20 seconds, then flap the covers up and down, releasing a little surprise. If the answer is no, your relationship has not gotten to the point when you should even be thinking about love. If your answer is yes and your man has not left you, then there's a good chance he's in love.

When a woman declares her love what she literally is saying is, "You are my soul mate, my reason for being. Without you I would be lost. I will lay down my life for you." A woman's love is like that Bounty quicker picker upper: It's bigger, wider, and sturdier, and it's more absorbent. And some women can fall in love at the drop of a *sombrero*. He puts his arm around your shoulder, and you get goose bumps. We should not use such events as a love thermometer. Just because he didn't try to sleep with you on the first date, or just because he took you to a nice restaurant, doesn't qualify you for a shot of Cupid's arrow in your ass. It reminds me of that game show, "Name that Tune," or in this case, "Love That Man."

"Alex, I can fall in love with that man in . . . ten minutes."

"Alex, I can fall in love with that man in . . . five minutes."

"Okay, Sharwanda, there's five minutes on the clock—love that man!"

#2   WHAT YOU HEARD:
"LET'S BE FRIENDS."

What she really said: "Don't touch me, let's only call each other periodically, and please stop calling me 'Babycakes.' And please return all of my stuff, but I'm keeping the necklace you gave me."

I don't think I have ever heard a man utter those words unless he is trying to pick you up. I really believe that saying is reserved for women only. It's used to let men down easy when the relationship starts feeling like cramps. You know they're coming, and you'd do anything to get rid of them.

#3   WHAT YOU HEARD:
"LET'S GET TOGETHER."

What he really said: If he's staring at a part of your anatomy that could be associated with (a) those "milk does a body good" commercials, (b) KFC, or (c) another name for a donkey (breasts, legs or ass), he probably means he wants to "get together" in the biblical sense.

Some men are quick to say, "You led me on . . . you teased me." So the next time he says "Let's get together," be sure to finish the sentence with "and do what?"

When a woman wants to "get together," she normally means she wants to spend some quality time with you. And if a man says okay, she'll show up at six a.m. spry and fully awake, with a picnic basket in hand, a change of clothes, tickets to the Frankie Beverly & Maze concert, and a gourmet dinner waiting at home once you finish the day's activities. And if you can only spend twenty-three out of the twenty-four hours in the day with her, she will be mad.

#4   WHAT YOU HEARD:
"MARRY ME."

What he really said: If he's under thirty . . . "I'm tired of doing my own laundry and cooking for myself and think of how much money we could save in rent." If he's over thirty . . . "I've sowed my oats. I know what I want. I'm looking for a life partner, and I'm ready to spend the rest of my life with you if you'll have me."

Now don't get me wrong, not every man who's over thirty has matured and reached this higher plane. And not all 20-somethings are looking for a maid. You must take other things into consideration, like if he has a steady job, his past track record, if he has a steady job. These things are very important. More important, do you love him and are you compatible, and does he have a steady job?

Women only mouth those words in an act of desperation. "Look here, we've been dating for eight years, now either shit or get off the pot." Some women are no longer waiting to hear that long-awaited, ten-million-dollar question. And even though we would much rather be the askee than the asker, when things get tight, we feel we have nothing to lose. Some of us even go so far as to get down on bended knee!

Now, for those men who give dogs a bad name, they will say anything to make you stay with them because usually they know they've messed up. These men can convince a homeless man to give up his last quarter. They're slick, but you can learn to read between the lines.

#5   WHAT YOU HEARD: "I NEED YOU."

What he really said: "I need you to tell my wife I wasn't with you last night."

Men tend to make this proclamation when they're knee-deep in doo-doo. You want to break up because it slipped his mind that he's married or maybe it's been eleven years and you still haven't met his mother—who lives next door! Unless he utters the words "I need you" in a life-threatening situation—like he's hanging off the side of a cliff and he needs you to pull him to safety—he's lying. Ladies, we can't allow ourselves to be human oxygen tanks for these men who continue to blow hot air. The next time he tells you he needs you, refer him to 911.

With women, it's an entirely different definition. I can spot a needy woman in a heartbeat. The topic of conversation is always men. She's clingy when she has a man. She's desperate and unhappy when she doesn't have one. Her hobbies and interests are whatever his hobbies and interests are, and she would rather die than be without him. I had a friend complete these sentences just to test her "need" factor. She failed miserably.

I feel happiest when *I'm with a man*.
I hate when *I'm without a man*.
I depend on *a man* to make me happy.
What I want people to remember most about me is that I *need a man*.

Secure women have a more practical meaning when they say "I need you." "I need you to move the furniture, set my VCR, take the garbage out, and change the oil in the car. And while you're at it, kill that icky spider, too!" Women aren't called the weaker sex for nothing. While a lot of women pride themselves on being independent, we do like to have a man around to do all the physical stuff that we can't, or don't want to do.

#6 WHAT YOU HEARD: "SHE DIDN'T MEAN NOTHING."

What he really said: "She's got it going on, and she treats me special like you used to. I'm just sorry I got busted."

If she didn't mean "nothing" you wouldn't be having this conversation. Some men are going to cheat. One of my male friends calls it "the drums syndrome." Come again, Kim? Well, according to my friend Dwayne, "Black men are prone to cheat because of this incessant drum that they hear in their heads that is coming from Mother Africa. Some African cultures apparently believe in polygamy. When a man takes a new wife there is a ceremony that involves the beating of drums, which black men in the States are somehow in tune with." That's a hell of a long-distance service, huh? Now, I forgot to ask whether he was sure those were drums or whether they were just plain dumbbells, because that's what he must have thought I was to fall for a line like that—again.

Well, how do I know if my man is cheating, Kim? If he says he's going to take the dog out for a walk and doesn't come back for three hours, and you don't even have a dog, that's a tell-tale sign. Or a more subtle hint might be he got tickets to a Toni Braxton concert, but he's going to take one of his boys. Yeah, right. If your man steps out on you, this would be a good time to reevaluate the relationship. I mean one can make a mistake; it happens. But two mistakes and I'm out. That's my rule: You get one chance to screw me. Well, you know what I mean. "Aw, baby, you cold, why don't you give a brother another chance?" This ain't baseball—no three strikes and you're out here.

When a woman says "He doesn't mean nothing," she really means just that: "I just wanted to make you jealous, with the hope that you would pay more attention to me." "Jeopardy" and "Wheel of Fortune" don't have nothing on women, 'cuz some of us can play serious games when it comes to dealing with men. Instead of just telling her man she needs more attention, a woman will send some flowers to herself and tell her boyfriend, "Thank you for the flowers." Of course he won't know what she's talking about, and he's liable to get so jealous he won't be able to see straight.

Jealousy is one way to get a man to react, but playing games can sometimes backfire. For instance, if you thank your man for the flowers you sent yourself and he says, "You're welcome, baby. I was hoping you would like them," look how ya' lookin!

#7   WHAT YOU HEARD: "IT'S NOT WHAT YOU THINK."

What he really said: "It's worse."

Whenever a man can form those words while making love to your best friend as you just happen to come home early, there is a serious misinterpretation going on. Well, ok, maybe the situation is not that extreme. Maybe it was the way his receptionist took his *dictation*. Or maybe it's those scratches on his back that could only be made by a pair of Lee Press Ons—and yours popped off months ago. Just like the prosecutors who represented the police officers who beat Rodney King, some men will ask you not to believe your lying eyes. And I say to you, don't believe his lying *ass*. Go with your first instinct. Now, if you're known to have a jealous instinct, don't be too quick to pass judgment. We got enough brothers in jail, so you don't want to convict an innocent man. Then again, you don't want to take as much time as that damn O.J. trial either. You need to consider your man's record, his motive, and his opportunity to do the deed—whatever that deed may be.

With women, "It's not what you think" generally means it's not what you think. Going back to that jealousy thing, men can see you talking with a guy and automatically think you want to take him home and have wild sex. My ex-boyfriend once saw me enjoying a conversation with a male friend at a party. He didn't talk to me during the whole ride home. He told me later that he felt that I really liked the guy. My body language gave it away. He said because I was shifting from one leg to another when I was talking to him was a sure sign I was attracted to him. He pointed out that I shifted the same way when I first met him. "I always shift when I'm bored," I explained. Have you ever seen a man look relieved and hurt at the same time?

#8   WHAT YOU HEARD: "I'LL CHANGE."

What he really said: "I'll lie."

If he looks like a f—k up, walks like a f—k up, and acts like a f—k up, he's a f—k up. People don't change unless they want to. If he says he'll change, don't believe him. Wait until the money is in the bank before you cash that lie. Think about it. When was the last time you tried to change something about yourself? Maybe you were going to quit smoking. Or not eat so many sweets. Or maybe not gossip so much. The problem is, you like doing these things. They make you happy. What's life without a few vices? Men are the same way. When they are walking down the street with you, they like staring at other women like they just got out of prison. If another man stares at you, they like getting into a fistfight to defend what's theirs. You have to decide whether or not you can tolerate his obsession with the game of football, or his insatiable appetite for making love to other women, or the way he shovels his food in his mouth like a bulldozer. And remember, if you require that your man change, you simply are requiring him to lie to you.

On the flip side, a woman normally means, "I'll change . . . my clothes." Some men have the tendency to want their women to look a certain way when they're out in public with them. What she might think is acceptable, he finds too short or too revealing or not short enough (especially if your man is your pimp), depending on what kind of man you have. Seldom does a woman have to profess to change her bad habits, because women are pretty darn perfect!

Nine Ways to Detect a Communication Breakdown in Your Relationship

1. You tell him you need some space. He makes some room in his closet for your things.

2. She tells you the relationship is over unless you give her a ring. You hang up and call her right back.

3. You tell him to bring home a tasty treat, so he brings home a hooker.

4. You tell her you want to see more of her, so she gains fifteen pounds.

5. She tells you she wants to start seeing other people. You get her a subscription to *People* magazine.

6. You tell him you need him to be more expressive sexually. He tells you he's been sleeping with your sister.

7. You suggest the two of you take a trip. She pushes you down the stairs and hollers, "Heads up!"

8. You remind him that your birthday is coming up, and he says, "Whatever."

℞. He says tomato, you say to-mah-to. He's says potato, you say banana.

Pick (me) Up (off the floor) Lines (when I finish laughing)

Why is it when some men see a woman for the first time and decide they want to get to know her, they come up with the lamest of all lines in all the universe? This one guy actually used the ancient line "You got some fries to go along with that shake?" Well, I guess that doesn't count. That was a homeless person I met in a McDonald's parking lot. I bought him a shake and he wanted some of my fries too. But, this other guy came up to me and said, "If I divorce my wife, would you become my woman?" He was serious, and got mad when I told him I had to think about it.

Now, I have to give it to the men who are bold enough to even attempt to make contact because like I said earlier, a woman, due to sheer cowardice, most times, will not approach a man she wants to meet. It's just that sometimes men try a little too hard. It's like when they let those stupid things come out of their mouths, I want to swipe them with a giant bottle of Wite-Out and tell them, "Next time, when you approach me, don't come with a tired line. Next time you come correct." Here are a few examples of lines we *hate*:

♥ **"Can I be your best friend?"** Where do men come up with these lines? Ok, it's a lot better than that tired "Hey, baby, can I go with you?" But really, what are men thinking? I could have the personality of an ant, but they want to be my best friend. The next time a guy asks you if he could be your best friend, give him your grocery list and your laundry ticket and see how fast he runs.

 "Is your man treating you right?" So what if he isn't? Do you suggest I trade him in for a loser like you who could come up with such a weak line? Please.

 "Hey, beautiful." Wow, now there's an original. If you want him to leave you alone, your response should be, "Hey, gruesome." That will stop him in his tracks.

 "Marry me." Bite me. Now what if I had a justice of the peace around the corner and my wedding dress in the trunk of my car? You never know what state of mind a sistah might be in. She might take you up on the offer. If she's smart, that line tells her exactly what kind of person you are: shallow. Women definitely want to hear those magical words, but let it be after we get to know you—ok?

 "Fuck you then, bitch." Now that's sure to impress me. Spoilsport.

The best line I have ever heard was simply when a man walked up to me, smiled, looked into my eyes and not at my breasts, and said, "Excuse me, I hope I'm not being presumptuous, you may have a husband and children at home, but I find you attractive and was wondering if you would care to meet me for lunch sometime." My response: "Yes, shall we go now?"

♥

Let's Talk
About Sex

One of the coolest things about being able to write your own book is that you can talk about whatever you want to talk about, whenever you want to talk about it. Of course, there has to be some logical and natural sentence structure and placement, but for the most part you can talk about anything. And since this is a book about relationships between men and women, and generally men and women have contact that leads to what I'm about to talk about now, it just seems fitting to talk about what I have been wanting to address for some time because of its significance in female and male relationships.

While I don't put as much weight on it as communication, which is why the communication chapter precedes this chapter, I will say this particular activity is crucial for the development of a healthy relationship. Then again, I guess it could have been addressed in the communication chapter. I mean, it is a type of nonverbal communication.

Though some find the subject quite awkward and personal, I feel it's something that everyone is curious about and thinks about at least as much as I do. Not to say that I think about it a lot, but I would say it is on my mind sometimes. So without beating around the bush, like I find most books do in an attempt to avoid this matter, and without putting off today what I can say tomorrow, I'm going to attempt to address this subject in a manner that I feel will be thought-provoking and tasteful whenever possible—"Let's Talk About Sex." Whew! Thank you, Salt N' Pepa for coming up with such a catchy song to make the rather difficult transition.

Growing Pains

Ever since elementary school, I was always curious about the whole sex thing. It probably had to do with the fact that I started my menstrual cycle at such a young age. I was ten. Unlike my friend Alma, who shouted, "Oh look, cherry Kool-Aid!" when she got hers, I was a little more aware of what was going on. I had my mother to thank for sitting me down and giving me the Cliff Notes version of the birds and the bees. Then after our talk, she handed me my own little "period starter kit," equipped with all kinds of neat stuff, including assorted sanitary napkins, tampons, and floral-scented vaginal wipes. I kept it under my bed and checked it *periodically,* and dreamt about the day when I would become a woman. I somehow had a romantic notion of the whole concept and really looked forward to it, except I had no idea how much responsibility it would entail.

Two days before it happened, I remember feeling really irritated. My little brother rolled over my toe with his Tonka truck, and my mother had to tear me off of him. I was watching "Sesame Street," and all of a sudden I had the urge to kick Big Bird's ass. He was just too damned friendly and yellow, all of the time. Then my stomach began to ache, like that time I ate a whole box of Fruity Pebbles in one sitting. And then it happened. I started bleeding from down yonder for the next three days, and there wasn't anything romantic about it.

My mother celebrated like I had won the national spelling bee competition. "Oh, Kimmy, you're a woman now. You have the power to give the gift of life!" It was quite a sight when my mother carted me off to school with all of my necessities. "Here you go, Kimmy. Here's your Barbie, don't forget your Scooby lunch box . . . oh, and I put some maxi-pads in there too. Try to remember to change them after you have your milk and cookies. Oh, and don't forget to take your children's aspirin with your milk."

By age 11, I still wasn't convinced that I had discovered my womanhood, even though I had the period thing down. Sex was a different story. The way we treated the subject was the way we treated our crazy uncle: We never talked about it, and pretty much agreed that it never existed. For the longest time I thought sex was the number after five.

I couldn't wait until high school because that's when they taught sex education. Mrs. Sanchez, our Puerto Rican health education teacher, was the most popular woman in the school.

She wore so much makeup, she could have been the poster adult for Maybelline. She always wore tight red dresses and big, glittery earrings, and she could roll her tongue and make that RRRRR sound, which was something I couldn't do to save my life. More than that, though, she was known for telling it like it was, and using a lot of visual aids!

On the first day of class, I walked into her classroom prepared to leave a woman. I was finally going to get all of my questions answered, like, if there was a G spot, why weren't there A, B, C, D, E, and F spots? And could you really get pregnant just from French kissing? And why were seamen so important when it came to making babies? Did it have to do with being out on the ships so long?

I was ready to learn all about the true meaning of a healthy sexual relationship. Unfortunately for me, Mrs. Sanchez had done such a good job teaching health education, the administration reassigned her to teach chemistry. Ms. Shapiro was Mrs. Sanchez's replacement.

Ms. Shapiro was at least 105, wore cat's-eye glasses, wool sweaters, and socks up to her chin, and reportedly rode to work each day on a broom. What I got, along with every other pimple-faced, sex-on-the-brain virgin adolescent, was how *not* to get pregnant, how *not* to get a venereal disease, how *not* to have, talk about, or enjoy sex. It was quite disappointing. And so I learned about sex the way almost every other girl did: I went away to college—a place where higher learning and raging hormones collide.

Going away to school is sheer freedom. The trouble you can get into is endless. You have your own room, no adult supervision, flexible class schedule, and a captive audience of members of the opposite sex. While I was successful at resisting the temptations and traps college men set to get in my panties (my going-away present from my parents was a personalized chastity belt), many of my sistah friends got caught in the web—and the information superhighway wasn't in existence then, so I'm not talking about the Internet.

Sabrina's story was hands down the saddest story I knew. Sabrina was one of my college roommates. We got along like sisters, and we had so much in common, she could have been me and I could have been her. We had similar backgrounds, we liked the same things, we had some of the same classes, and we thought alike.

After a day of celebrating because we had both aced our psychology exams, we decided to check out the Friday night Student Union Mixer. Our first college party! A popular junior named Reggie scooped Sabrina up right away, and they danced for an hour, non-stop. Then he invited her back to his frat house.

"Are you crazy? Do you think I'm some dumb little freshman? Is that what you think I am? Well, think again."

Reggie was surprised by her sass. It seemed to make him like her even more. "Oh, I will have you, that's unquestionable."

"Yeah, right!" We laughed all the way back to the dorm.

Early the next morning, the front desk receptionist patched the downstairs intercom into our room. "Sabrina, there is a gentleman visitor for you."

"Who is it?"

Who else, but Reggie. He came to escort her to class, which he promised to do every day for the rest of her college career. He was there waiting for her after class bearing that Cheshire cat grin. He showed up in the library, the cafeteria, lecture hall, and yes, the dorm, every morning, as he had promised, and every morning Ms. Lucy would announce him on the intercom, "Sabrina, there is a gentleman visitor here to see you." And then Reggie started showing up in Sabrina's dreams.

She confided in me three months later that she really liked him a lot, even thought she was falling in love with him. Like a good mother, I gave her my blessing, but told her to take it slow. After all, he had a reputation on campus for being a ladies' man. She explained he wasn't like that with her, that when they got together they talked and laughed mostly. She admitted they had kissed a couple of times, but she stopped it before things went too far. She felt like he had become her best friend, which made me feel like chopped liver, but I was happy for her.

Then one day, he invited us to the frat house for a party. I declined as I had my cafeteria work-study job I had to attend to. I don't know why they called them work-study because you damn sure didn't have time to study in between mopping floors and cleaning up spilled milk. Anyway, Sabrina went to the party, got drunk, and lost her innocence to Reggie, the supposed love of her life. She cried to me later, and confessed that it was painful. She did not enjoy it at all. And then, when I thought things couldn't get any worse, she told me that when it was over, Reggie whispered in her ear, "I told you I would have you." After that night he never called on her again. Like a skilled hunter, he had stalked her, captured her, devoured her, and like a carjacker, left her stunned and having to walk home. She dropped out of school the next year.

My friend Geneva, whom I also met in college, must have been sleeping or out to lunch because she didn't discover sex in college. As a matter of fact, she hasn't discovered sex yet. She is a thirty-one-year-old virgin. Isn't that amazing? Sometimes I want to slap her, and other times I feel like I should be worshipping her and throwing rose petals at her feet or something. And you wouldn't believe the perks for being a virgin these days. You get to go to the front of the line, you get discount tickets at movie theaters, you don't have to pay taxes, feed parking meters, or obey traffic laws. She even makes a little extra money on the side by opening up her home, and her legs, as a tourist attraction. She just sits in the window for a couple of hours while her mom stands at the gate and collects the admission fee.

I wonder how many women would trade in all of their sexual encounters, both the wild torrid ones and the "is that it?" ones, to have their virginity back. Virginity was kind of nice. I remember feeling so innocent, so pure, so horny! Unfortunately, there's no going back, but thank God for abstention. It's kinda like when people become born-again Christians. When you decide to abstain from sex, you become a born-again virgin. Hey, it's the next best thing to being there!

Once I told a guy I was dating that I was abstaining from sex, and he replied, "How are we going to do it, if you're not here?" I believe he had a metal plate in his head. I just hope that when Geneva finally does decide to "open sesame," it will be worth the wait. And believe me, after thirty-one years, it's gonna take more than a notion to crack that nut.

I was surprised to learn that most women I talked to had disappointing first times. Disappointing like if at Christmas time, when you'd been dating the same guy for six years and hoping that you'd get an engagement ring, he bought you the "Richard Simmons' Yuletide Fun" video. Disappointing like if you had a date with Wesley Snipes but he had to cancel so he sent Raj from "What's Happening!!" in his place. No fireworks. No stars. No climax—even though a couple of women reported that their blood pressure did go up.

My first sexual experience, I have to say, was not disappointing. It was with my high school sweetheart. He was strong and handsome. He was on the football team. I was a twirler. It happened during our senior year. He was gentle and sweet, and he made that night wonderful and magical. Afterward, I had no regrets. Even though I must admit, choosing to lose my virginity on my living room couch, while my mother was sleeping in the next room, did not make for the best mood. I was deflowered on a flowered couch. How fitting.

A Time to Thrill

For the record, let me just say that I happen to think it is the most healthy and exciting thing that you can do. The rhythmic pumping, sweat dripping, muscles contracting. But the most enjoyable part is when my trainer takes that damn heavy weight off of my chest, and I can breathe a little.

Seriously, I believe sex is the most pleasurable experience a person can have. I mean how many things can you do, legally, that can give you a feeling of pure bliss? Playing sports, eating your favorite meal and not having to worry about the calories, quenching your thirst after running a marathon—it's all that, wrapped into one. Pure, unmitigated bliss!

On occasion when I'm at some boring gathering, to amuse myself I watch men and wonder what it must be like to be intimate with them. Can you imagine what it must be like to be with Spike Lee? I can see him using his little portable ladder to climb on top of me, "Come on baby, do the right thing! Do the right thing!"

When I'm in a relationship, I admit I look forward to making love. I try to wait a respectable amount of time, but I'm not one of these women who waits so long to give a man some that his head swells up. I mean what's the purpose of baking a cake and then not eating it? It's like when you buy some new clothes, and you can't wait to get home and try them on. You want to see how they look on you, how they feel against your skin.

It's amazing how gentle and obedient a man can become when he's making love. It's like your stuff is kryptonite. To hear a man call my name in the most passionate, loving way, as if he were saying, "Oh, Kim, all that matters is you and what you're doing with me right now!" That's a remarkable talent to be born with, don't you think?

Another reason I love making love is I love men. I think I must have been a gay man in a former life. I love the way a man walks, the way he moves, the way he smells. Some men have a certain scent that turns me on instantly. I love how neatly our bodies fit together, like two Lego pieces. The way his large hands hold me and touch my body. His delicious lips caressing my shoulders. The mere anticipation of him entering me is enough to make me explode. . . . Excuse me for a minute. . . .

As I was saying, there's nothing like making love, especially when a man enters the waiting love nest, and like a deejay, starts mixing until he finds the right rhythm. Maybe I'm weird but I don't have to have a lot of foreplay, like I think most women do. That's like going to a Luther Vandross concert just to see his opening acts. I mean foreplay is like the appetizer, it's nice, but it's not going to fill you up like the main course will. I guess a man just needs to find a happy medium. Or he could just ask, "Baby, are you ready for the main course?"

How You Can Tell if a Man Is a Good Lover

♂ Your vagina percolates when he walks into the room.

♂ He has his condoms custom made.

♂ He asks you if you want original or extra spicy.

♂ His phone number is the only one in your black book.

♂ He doesn't need to use his hands when putting on a condom.

♂ He has guard rails on his bed.

♂ You want seconds, and thirds, and fourths. . . .

The Big Thang Theory

Ode to the Penis

The male appendage, how I love thee.

You perform so many functions—oh, do you have to pee?

The penis, the penis, it is so great!

It is upon the penis that I will pontificate.

The penis, the penis, there's none can compare.

It has its own hat, and its own head of hair.

My little pussycat is your best friend.

'Cuz you always stand up for what you believe in.

Like a little soldier, all ready for war.

C'mon, Big Daddy, I'm beggin' for more.

I really do think the penis is an amazing piece of machinery. What other part of the human anatomy is both hard and soft? The skin is so smooth too. Women are spending a fortune in alpha hydroxy to get skin like this.

And it's not just beautiful, the penis is smart too. "Its got a mind of its own"—isn't that what men always say?

I think if I were a man, I would play with my penis all of the time. Really! Okay, maybe not all of the time, but every now and then. I would definitely whip it out and pee on people I didn't like. I would use it as a pointer to give directions. I would even use it as a paperweight. That's why God made me a woman, so I wouldn't become a pervert.

I would be a liar if I said the size of a penis is not important. I like for a man to be packing, but I don't want him necessarily to be "over-packed." Nor do I care for a man who only "has a little overnight bag." I don't know any woman who is really overjoyed when a man takes off his clothes and she sees he's hung like a horse. That expression men think is pure joy is actually sheer horror. What we are really thinking is, "Doesn't he know the buffalo is extinct, and I am definitely going to be having a headache tonight." The theory Bigger is Better does not apply when it comes to this appendage. Biceps, triceps, yes.

What is more important than the size of a man's penis is the size of his heart—followed by the size of his penis.

Great SEXpectations

Sex by itself is not necessarily that complicated. Yes, there are a lot of things to consider: his penis size, wondering if will it hurt, his penis size, dying, the revealing of the cellulite, his penis size. And to top it off he could be on top of you, doing things to your body that don't seem humanly possible. But once you can get past all of that, the actual act can be simple.

Because women's feelings are as fragile as those paper toilet seat covers you find in public restrooms, making love tends to mean so much more to us. We have given him the ultimate gift and therefore, in return, we expect: his respect, his devotion, his undying love, a commitment, him to pay our rent, a diamond ring, a year's supply of hair care products. A girl can dream, can't she?

Most men don't have to have a reason to have sex. The mere fact that they have that sensitive piece of equipment attached to the front of their bodies is reason enough. And their only expectation afterward might be for you to tiptoe when you leave so you won't wake them.

I had a conversation with an older woman who gave me a totally different perspective on sex. Her philosophy was "Life is like a box of dildos. You never know which one will turn you on." She warned me of the dangers of thinking that when you lie down with a man, it means he owes you something.

If You Sleep with a Man, It Does Not Necessarily Mean . . .

 you should start picking out china patterns.

 he wants you to meet his parents.

♥ he wants you.

♥ he's going to leave his wife.

 you can drive his Benz.

♥ you're actually going to sleep.

When I'm with a new partner, I get as excited and nervous as a white woman in an elevator full of black men. Seriously, it's like embarking on a fascinating new research project: While you're hopeful that the final outcome will produce the desired results, you can't always guarantee that your hypothesis will be proven.

For one thing, once you unwrap the packaging, you might be dealing with damaged goods. He could take off his clothes and have the body of an underdeveloped little boy.

Second, even if he has the right tools, he might not know how to use them properly. To avoid any accidents, you might find you have to attach traffic signs to certain parts of your anatomy, like EXIT ONLY, or SLIPPERY WHEN WET.

And finally, it just might be a case where your tests are inconclusive. No matter how hard you try to get that loving feeling, you realize that, for some strange reason, you just aren't sexually compatible. It's like trying to fit a square peg in a round hole. (Now *would* be an appropriate time to have your mind in the gutter.)

Too many men approach making love all wrong. Some men think women are like Pavlov's dogs—just ring our bell, and we'll produce the desired response. But a stimulus doesn't always elicit the correct response, especially if the stimulus is you sucking on my breast like you're drinking a thick chocolate milk shake through a straw. That hurts!

I was listening to LL Cool J's "Doin' It" song the other day. You know the one, "Doin it, doin' it, and doin' it well." I mean, the woman is quite convincing with her moans and groans, but I knew she was really thinking "fakin' it, and fakin' it, and fakin' it well." All women have done a little play acting, some being full-fledged drama queens when it comes to "doin' it." Oh, I can hear it now. Men who are reading this are saying, "Oh, you're crazy, ain't no woman ever faked it with me. Kim, you just ain't been loved the right way." Every man thinks they can come in and be a pinch hitter when it comes to making love to a woman. Sometimes women would prefer you to be a "no batter" because the truth is, a lot of men don't know the first thing about hitting a homerun.

A woman told me her boyfriend was such a lousy lover, she could only muster up enough energy to make love when the mood was right. I asked her what did she consider the right mood. She said it was normally on an odd-numbered day, when she had gotten a good night's sleep the night before, there was a high tide, an eclipse was on the horizon, and she didn't feel bloated.

I think if it were up to women, when it came to lousy lovers, we would prefer to bottle up all of the bad sexual encounters with the man and instead make intercourse a once-a-year thing—like a national holiday. We would call it Intimate Day. That way, maybe it would be something to look forward to.

Ten Biggest Turn-on Myths

1. *If I pinch her nipples real hard, she will come quicker.*
   Contrary to popular belief, squeezing a woman's nipple until all of the color drains from her face is not a turn on. It can hurt so good only to a point. I believe the philosophy "no pain, no gain" does not apply when it comes to these sensitive puppies.

2. *If I rub her clitoris like I'm polishing silverware, she will come quicker.*
   Just because you've struck gold and found the mother of all erogenous zones doesn't mean you have to then start treating it like you're excavating. Again, this is a

very tender spot on a woman, that should be handled with gentle, loving care. No woman wants to have blisters on her stuff when you're through.

3. *If I come, she'll come.*
Some men think just because they're giving an "injection," that the medicine will start to kick in soon after. It doesn't work like that. My having an out-of-body experience is not contingent on whether you have one first. There is some work you have to do in between.

4. *If she's screaming at the top of her lungs, she's about to come.*
There could be a whole host of other reasons why she's screaming, like she's seen Urkel with no clothes on. For one, you might have entered through an "Exit Only" area. Or she just might be tired of your ass going nowhere fast, and she wants you to get up off of her.

5. *Having a ménage à trois with her best friend will make her come quicker.*
Having a ménage à trois with her best friend will make *you* come quicker! My best friend and I share a lot of things, but looking at a man butt-naked, thinking he is about to get a two-for-one, is an experience I do not care to partake in. Now, I understand there are women out there who like to ride on the kinky side of the road. I personally choose to stay out of the carpool lane when it comes to sex.

6. *Putting my tongue in her ear will make her come quicker.*
I don't know anyone who likes that wet, spongy feeling. For one thing, it feels wet and spongy, and another

thing, just like anything that's placed close to the ear, sound amplifies and gives you that horrible feedback noise. Besides, once he sticks his tongue in your ear, you're not even thinking about sex, you're concentrating on when would be the best time to wipe your ear out.

7. *If I ram her like they do with those cars when they test crash dummies, she'll come quicker.*
News flash. Your penis is not a sledgehammer and I am not a slab of concrete. Some men think in order for a women to get maximum satisfaction, they have to stick it in until they reach her tonsils. Problem is, her tonsils have been out for two years. Women like to be stroked like a fine violin. Bouncing up and down like a pogo stick is not going to get it. Quit drilling for oil, Jed Clampett!

8. *A woman is always ready.*
Just because your penis can stand at attention in a matter of milliseconds, doesn't mean a woman's body operates the same way. Some women need a little more preparation before you go entering the sugar walls. A little foreplay would be nice. And yes, if possible, we would like to be awake.

9. *Performing oral sex on a woman will make her come quicker.*
This all depends on how it's done. If you treat it like a gourmet meal that you want to savor before tasting, then you might be on the right track. But if you treat it like fast-food take-out, you might as well get your head out from under the table and stick to what you know.

18. *Standing on her head will make her come quicker.*
I'm as limber as the next person, but come on. Trying it in different positions is fun, but if you need to shout a set of instructions at me during the process—"Here, put your leg up here, grab my ankle, scoot down three feet"— I feel like I'm playing Twister! Keep it simple.

Women are partly to blame for why some men think they deserve a gold medal after sex when, truthfully, they didn't even make it past the finals. Unless he comes out and asks you, there's really no proper protocol when it comes to letting a man know that he did not light your fire. It's too uncomfortable and awkward to talk about, especially if he couldn't even get the charcoal lit.

Wouldn't it be convenient if, after sex, you could call a man's 1-800-HOW DID I DO? number and let him know? Better yet, what if a man just gave you a comment card, like you find in some restaurants. You could complete it at your leisure, taking time to be thorough and reflective, and then just drop it in the mail. An example is on the next page.

Sexcapades

It's amazing how some men will use sex to act out their own little fantasies. I think in the beginning they do it to please us, but then they get carried away. My friend was telling me about a guy she dated. Greg was a pretty big guy who had a hell of an appetite. I'm not talking about for sex, he loved to eat— food. She said it was not unusual for him, during foreplay, to pull out a bottle of whipped cream or caramel, spread it over

Sexual Performance Comment Card

♥

1. How was the overall service you received tonight?

EXCELLENT   GOOD   FAIR   POOR

2. How long before he came?
5–10 seconds (He hadn't even gotten his pants off.)
15–20 minutes (He was very efficient.)
I don't know (I kept falling asleep.)

3. How long did you have to wait before you came?
5–10 seconds (Rubbing my legs together in my tight jeans did the trick.)
15–20 minutes (He was very efficient.)
I'm still waiting.

4. Please rate the following:

His foreplay techniques	**EXCELLENT**	**GOOD**	**FAIR**	**POOR**
His maneuvers	**EXCELLENT**	**GOOD**	**FAIR**	**POOR**
His gentleness	**EXCELLENT**	**GOOD**	**FAIR**	**POOR**
His odor	**EXCELLENT**	**GOOD**	**FAIR**	**POOR**
His flexibility	**EXCELLENT**	**GOOD**	**FAIR**	**POOR**
His bathroom	**EXCELLENT**	**GOOD**	**FAIR**	**POOR**

5. Will you continue to patronize what has been established?

YES   NO   MAYBE

6. How can the service be improved?

_____

_____

her body, and lick until it made him hungry. He would stop and look at her as if he'd forgotten what he was doing, and say, "Baby, let's order a pizza from Antonio's." It would get so bad that some days he would have every non-perishable item from his kitchen cabinet in the bedroom. Finally, they just started doing it in the kitchen. This ritual continued to escalate until one day she came over and he said, "Hey, I got a surprise for you tonight. Go look in the bedroom." Lying on the side of his bed were all the fixings needed for a submarine sandwich. Smack dab in the middle of the bed was a giant piece of bread! She suddenly felt like she was dating Jeffrey Dahmer. That's when she realized the man had lost his fool mind.

And what about talking in bed? Take Fred, for example. He was the big, strong, silent type. The only way I knew he was conscious was I could hear him breathing. The silence was so unbearable at times that I would ask, "Do you like this?" and he would simply nod his head. It got to the point where my sole purpose in our lovemaking was to make him say something. When I finally got him to say "Oh, baby!" I jumped up and shouted, "Yes!!!!" The only thing was, we were both fully clothed. Now I want you. Talk to me, Daddy—but watch what you say.

The Biggest Turn-off Phrases to Hear When Making Love

"WHO'S PUSSY IS THIS?"

For some reason, probably because the white man won't let them own nothing else in society, brothers have a need to possess the pussy while making love. Men should be careful before asking such questions because some women just might tell them the truth. "Who's pussy is this? What the hell kind of question is that? It's mine, fool." Instead we lie, "It's yours, baby. It's all yours."

"DO ME."

Come again? Do me. Could you be a little more vague and a lot less romantic??? Do what, exactly? Do a Lorena Bobbitt on your ass is what we feel like doing when we hear some crap like that. Or sometimes you might not even get that splendid pleasantry. A push or a nudge of your head southward-bound might be what he contends is enough for you to get the picture, so you can get to lickin' the love Popsicle. *Stop!* Just keep in mind, once she gives, she may be expecting to receive. And if a woman wants to "do you," she'll do it in her own time. So enough with the pleasantries.

"WHAT'S MY NAME?"

What's your name? What, you don't remember? Seriously, men, get off the macho wagon. My friend told me about how her boyfriend wanted her to shout out his name when she climaxed. After about six months of being intimate, he asked why she never honored his request. I suppose you can figure out the answer to that one.

Men, really, in the throes of passion, we *are not* trying to take a test! We're trying to get our groove on. Now what if, for some reason, we accidentally call you Denzel when your name is Pookie. Then you get all mad. The next time a man asks you something like that, tell him to be like the military: Don't ask, and you won't tell.

"LET ME HIT IT."

I know my love is intoxicating, but do I really look like a joint? "Hitting it" doesn't come close to what I want you to do to "it." A little foreplay first would be nice. Not "Oh the basketball game's over, I'm buzzed from that forty—come here and let me hit it!" You hit a baseball—you make love to a woman. Next time he gives you that line, tell him he can hit it all right. Hit the door and don't look back.

Love Thyself

I couldn't talk about sex unless I addressed the subject of loving oneself. If you need to release some tension and there isn't anyone around, you may have to take care of business the old-fashioned way, if you get my drift. Of course, I mean masturbation. It is natural and it is your body and there is nothing to be ashamed of. And ignore the myth that if you do this perfectly natural act hair will grow on the palms of your hand. That's ridiculous.

You can buy all kinds of battery-operated devices and toys to help you out if necessary. But I suggest doing it in the privacy of your own home. You don't want to be riding the bus to work and there is a hum emanating from down there because you left something on. The great thing about masturbation is you know you are going to be faithful to you and you are going to be good to you. So reach out and touch yourself. Now, excuse me—you start the next chapter; for some strange reason, I have to go shave my palms.

♥

Check Yourself, Before You Wreck Yourself

Sometimes I think God has a problem with women. I mean look at the kind of time He put into creating us in the first place. Can you imagine the trauma Eve must have felt knowing she came from one lonely little rib? She didn't have anyone to give her those mother-daughter talks, she had a father who thought He knew everything, and her lover was out every night hanging with the monkeys and lions. If I were her, I probably would have been kicking it with a snake too, 'cuz you know they didn't have cable.

And think about all the pain we have to endure compared to our counterparts. Menstrual pain, birthing pain, making love pain. I mean, you never hear men saying, "Ouch, you're hurting me." They might say, "Hurt me, baby. Hurt me." But they're usually referring to a good kind of hurt. Our pain is real. Have you noticed how men can reproduce damn near until they drop dead, and a woman's curfew is around fortysomething—unless you're Diana Ross?

It's a She Thing

I don't think that it's a coincidence women are made the scapegoat for everything from banishment from paradise to the breakdown of the family. We're getting blamed because we want to be productive citizens and 'cuz we like a little fruit. Ain't that a bitch!

Despite God's apparent favoritism toward men, I have to admit, we often do ourselves in, especially when dealing with the opposite sex. Women can bring so much baggage into relationships, men think they're going on a seven-day cruise. And we have more mood swings than Dennis Rodman has hair colors. Of course, we always have that convenient excuse: "I'm sorry I snapped your head off...I have my period." Or "I didn't mean to call you a lying rat-faced bastard...I'm premenstrual." I had a boyfriend who charted my mood changes for an entire six months before he discovered there were only two days out of the month that I wasn't on some cycle or going through some sort of phase.

Disappearing Tracks

Men also don't understand that women are very sensitive, highly complex creatures. Especially when it comes to our appearance. I think back in the day, men and women used to both play dress-up. Especially British and French royalty. Then, like Tag, all of a sudden women were "it." We got stuck having to wear makeup and high heels and dealing with our hair.

One day my friend was watching Toni Braxton's video "You're Makin' Me High" with her boyfriend when he turned to her and said, "Can you get your hair like that?"

"Yeah, for about fifteen hundred dollars and a whole lot of bags of synthetic hair!" she exclaimed.

"That's not her real hair?" he asked, dumbfounded.

Men can see a woman on television with a short hairdo one week, and the next week with flowing locks, and think the woman's hair grows fast. Her tracks could be as big as Big Foot's and he still wouldn't know. He'll notice, however, if you leave the house looking like Sinead O'Connor and come back with fifty pounds of hair down your back.

"I know you said you wanted to make a change, but damn!" That is not what women want to hear. A woman needs her man to be supportive of her new hairstyle. When she says, "Do you like it?" he shouldn't flinch or make a funny face. Even if she has a Don King thing happening, he should simply smile and say, "Yes." Even if she's overdone it, he should keep quiet and look on the bright side: During the winter months her hair can double as a comforter!

Let's Hear It from the Boy

Wouldn't you love to be a fly on your ex's wall, just to hear what he has to say about you? Men may not express their feelings very well while they are in a relationship—"Baby, I just don't think it's working out . . . I need some space"—but you better believe they gossip just like some women when they get with their boys. "Ah, man, let me tell you about this sorry heifer. . . ."

So, unless we read *Ebony Man* on a regular basis, or until the man's version of *Waiting to Exhale* is written, we can't be certain what they think about us. (I wonder what they would call the male version? *Damn, I Gotta Breathe* or *Gimme Some Air, Bitch!*)

I learned recently that men have as many complaints about us as we do about them. (My attorney let me read my ex-husband's deposition.) I also got an idea from talking to lots of men as part of the research I did for this book. (Oh, and I got a few phone numbers too!)

According to one of my male friends, a man likes a woman who is aggressive, but not too bossy; intelligent, but not too brainy; beautiful, but doesn't attract the attention of other men; and virgin-like, but an excellent lover. What can I say; this is from a man who drives an imported car with a MADE IN THE USA bumper sticker.

My other male friends couldn't come to a consensus on a woman's special qualities that give them that loving feeling. However, they were in agreement on the type of sistahs that could be packed up and shipped to the moon. The women they especially had disdain for are what I'll call 911 Women, "What's-Mine-Is-Mine-and-What's-His-Is-Mine" Ladies, Gullible Gals, "The-Clock-Is-Running-Out" Sistahs, and Superbitches.

"I've-Fallen-and-I-Can't-Get-Up" Women

I can always tell when my friend Lisa starts a new relationship. I never see her, I never hear from her, she puts her stuff in storage and moves in with the guy, and depending on whether or not his place allows dogs, Scruffy may wind up shaking in his doggie boots down at the pound.

Six months later, the calls start back regularly, she's ready to hang out again, she's trying to kick out the person she let sublet her apartment, and Scruffy gets a pardon . . . for now.

When I ask her what happened, she shrugs her shoulders and says, "I think my love was just too strong for him." Translation: Her love was just too suffocating.

Women like Lisa grow up believing that they are incomplete without a man. And when they meet someone, they immediately fall in love and get Alzheimer's about everybody and everything else because all that matters in life is their men. Like a dropped contact lens, they're afraid of losing them.

Just like a one-year-old baby, Lisa suffers from object permanence. Once her man is out of her sight, she thinks he's gone for good. She needs to be constantly reassured that he's coming back, even though he just went to pay the pizza delivery man. She becomes this very needy, helpless creature who all of a sudden forgets how to breathe without his assistance. She's like a parking meter: You have to continuously feed her to keep her happy. She has to be his number-one, -two, and -three priorities. He can't scratch his butt without getting her permission, and he might as well forget about playing sports with the fellas. If she can't play, he can't play.

I can see how a man would be flattered by all of the attention in the beginning. He thinks, "Wow, she really depends on me." But when she calls his boss and asks if it's possible for him to work from home, so that she can see more of him during the day, I can see how that would turn a brother off.

In the beginning of a relationship, it's only normal to want to be around each other. It's like the feeling you get when you're a kid on Christmas Eve, and you know you've been nice, for part of the year, anyway. Santa hadn't even made it up the chimney before my brother and I began ripping open our gifts. But unlike Christmas, which only comes once a year, a relationship is a day-to-day gig. You can see how that could become mundane. Especially if you're routinely on a person's jock. Eventually he's going to develop an itch. And inevitably you're going to get *scratched off*.

A person needs room to breathe, room to spread his wings, room to become his own person. Hell, a person needs room. I mean, how did you get through the night before he came into the picture?

Most men like independent women. That damsel in distress act played out right about the time Oprah and Clair Huxtable came on the scene. Find your own interests away from your man—and joining a support group for women who love too much does not count.

I am proud to say I have never had the need to be with a man 24/7. Okay, there were times when the sex was so good that I wished the penis were detachable, so I could keep it by my bedside for emergencies. But that was just wishful thinking.

You Know You're a Needy Woman If . . .

♥ "Me and My Shadow" is your theme song.

♥ you wear a patch on your arm to curb your addiction . . . to him.

♥ *Fatal Attraction* is your favorite movie.

♥ you have a special phone with only one preset number, his.

♥ you sign all of your love letters S.O.S.

♥ Linus is your favorite Peanuts character.

♥ he has to check in with you more times than Liz Taylor at the Betty Ford Clinic.

♥ you want to install Lojack on the inside of his underwear.

♥ you carry a hologram of him in your wallet.

Looking for Mr. Good Car

I was at the bank the other day, when I overheard these two women talking about a bad date one of them had the night before. "Girl, it was awful. He was wearing this played-out polo shirt with some Jordache jeans. His glasses were held together by some masking tape, and to top it off, he was driving a Yugo. I was too through. I mean he took me to a nice restaurant, and he was pretty interesting to talk to, but I told him wasn't nothing happening until he updated his wardrobe and got a better car."

Out of the corner of my eye, I could see that these were attractive women. They both had on their designer outfits and purses. Their hair was laid, their faces and nails were all done up. The sistahs had it going on. "Well, I guess they can afford to be picky," I thought to myself. Then the sistah doing the talking said, "Girl, I gotta go. Here comes my bus."

If I were a man, I would resent a woman whose first question out of her mouth when she met me was, "What kind of car do you drive?" What should that matter? It's not your car and even if you do end up *riding* in it, you will only be the *passenger*. When a nice car goes past, folks aren't breaking their necks looking at the passenger. I've never heard anyone say, "Ohh, that Porsche looks so nice wrapped around that woman sitting on the right." They might give the driver the once-over, but the passenger could be a sack of groceries for all they care.

If that woman would have taken one minute to look beyond what was in front of her, she might have discovered the man had a heart of gold. "Yeah, but is that gold 18-karat? And if so, can I cash it in and buy me a Lexus? I didn't think so."

I admit, I like nice things (just ask my interior decorator), but I don't expect anyone to buy anything for me. I'm far from one of those material girls who judge a man by his net worth or who are always trying to get a man who's got something. Why not get it for yourself? While you were expending all that energy to meet Mr. Rich, you probably stepped over a sack of money someone dropped on the curb, or forgot to check your Lotto number the day you were the million-dollar winner.

Some women say they want a *real* man but they base it on things that are synthetic. "He's got to be a nice dresser. His ride has got to be jamming, and he has to be making at least three times what I'm making." Okay, let's see, three times zero is zero. Isn't that right? Their full-time job is trying to find the goose that laid the golden egg. And that's why they keep coming up with . . . goose eggs.

I have always been dumbfounded by women who will sleep with a man just because he's a celebrity or professional athlete. These women are easy to spot. You can usually find them at an NBA basketball game wearing something so revealing you can see their reproductive organs. And when a player makes a basket, they're the ones screaming, "Yeah, touchdown!"

One day, my girlfriend Charisse and I were watching some movie with Wesley Snipes, and she said, "Oh, if I could just meet that man, I know I could get him to go home with me." I mean she wanted this man badly and it was just because he was a celebrity.

"For all you know, Charisse, he could go home at night and kick his woman's ass," I said.

"That's okay. As long as I was getting paid, and he was taking me out to those movie premieres, I wouldn't mind."

I am even more amazed at the women who will sleep with someone just because he is *associated* with a celebrity or professional athlete. I affectionately refer to these women as "eeny meeny mynie hoes." I knew this girl whose goal was to sleep with a member of this very popular singing group, so she slept with his stage hand. (His only responsibility was to plug in the equipment.) She explained to me later that, by sleeping with the stage hand, she was "stroking strategically." After the stage hand, she seduced the road manager, and then had hot sex with the bodyguard. Though she never quite made it to the singer, she was proud of the fact that she got pretty close. She told me she bedded the back-up singers right before the tour moved on to the next city. I didn't have the heart to tell her that Boyz II Men doesn't have back-up singers.

Goldie Diggins
627 Leech Drive
Anywhere, USA 90210

Career Objective
*Seeking an exciting opportunity to meet a man
who will set me up for life.*

Measurements
38"   breast*
24"   waist
36"   hips

HEIGHT: *How tall do you want me to be?*
EYES: *brown, green, or blue*

Education
Wilshire School of Beauty—B.A.

Experience[†]
1995–96—Makeup Artist to Dennis Rodman
1993–94—Montel Williams's Hair Stylist
1991–92—Dallas Cowboy Cheerleader
1986–88—Bobby Brown's Personal Assistant

Special Skills
I model, sing, and dance. I am very flexible and limber. I am also
a hit at parties.

Hobbies
Shopping, getting my nails done, attending basksetball, football,
and baseball games, being invited to exclusive parties where I
could possibly meet Shaquille O'Neal or Grant Hill.

*I will know my definite size next week. That's when I'm scheduled for my next
 breast implant surgery.
†Gaps in employment mean I found a financier during those periods.

Ten Ways to Tell if a Woman Is a Gold Digger

1. She has your house appraised before she agrees to go out with you.

2. Her motto is "Show me the money."

3. She's dated every member of the New York Knicks.

4. Robin Givens and Marla Maples-Trump are her idols.

5. She has a list of your assets attached to her refrigerator.

6. Instead of love, cherish, and obey, her wedding vows include "shop until you drop."

7. Her nickname for you is "Sugar Daddy."

8. She wears her prospector hat and carries her shovel on a date.

9. Her first question after asking your name is, "What's your bank account number?"

10. Her next question is, "Do you have a will?"

It Takes a Fool to Learn . . .

Dear Ebony Advisor: I am 22 and the man I am dating is also 22. We have been dating for three days. He has already slept with my mother and my brother. He says he is sorry and won't do it again. And says he loves me very much. I love him very much too, but that was not a very nice thing he did with my mother and brother. I am torn. Should I take him back?

— Confused in Colorado

How many times have you read the "Dear Ebony Advisor" column and just wanted to shake some sense into those women? You would think that putting something stupid like that down on paper, and then reading it back to yourself, would be enough to make you realize the obvious answer— drop-kick him.

I was listening to the radio the other day when one of the local deejays put a call out for women to phone in with their "waiting to exhale" stories. Some of the stories were incredible. One women had dated a guy for sixteen years before he finally proposed. She told him she needed more time. Talk about thinking things through.

Then it seemed there was story after story where women thought everything was going peachy keen in their respective relationships, and then all of a sudden, the grim reaper of love stole the guy's heart away like a purse snatcher.

Barbara, for instance, told of how she had been with her man eleven years. She was there for her man, helped pay his way through medical school, only for him to leave her for another woman. When the deejay asked what happened in the relationship, she replied, "I honestly don't know. I don't know what more I could have done. I'm a model, and I'm not bragging or anything but I've got an excellent body. So I don't know why he was trippin'." Hello! Was she kidding? I didn't hear her say anything about the two of them having a friendship or being able to communicate, etc. She apparently thought her good looks and her great body were the only prerequisites for a lasting relationship. I thought to myself, she should have used that money she spent to put him through school to buy herself a clue. I agree, we should support our men emotionally and financially to a certain extent, but support ain't never guaranteed a damn thing. Even a pair of support hose doesn't hang in there for the long run.

Thanks to the advent of tasteless talk shows, stupid women everywhere can be not only heard but seen. Now, don't get me wrong, I think sometimes talk shows are a good thing. They can be entertaining and informative. Most of the things I've learned about life I learned from watching talk shows. Seriously, like that compulsive behavior disorder. I never knew anything like that existed until I saw it on a talk show. Can you believe something like that exists? I can't believe something like that exists. It is absolutely amazing that something like that exists. Who would have thought in a million years something so freaky would exist? I'm telling you it's amazing that it exists.

Now what was I saying? Oh yeah, I was watching "Ricki Lake" the other day when she announced, "Today we're going to be talking to sistahs who suspect their men ain't being straight up." (Ricki kills me when she's trying to be down.) First, I checked the calendar to make sure it wasn't April Fool's Day. Then I watched as Ricki exposed my simple sistahs for all the world to see. The sad part was, a lot of them were grown women!

And it's cold sometimes how they do us. They call you up and tell you they would like you to be a guest on their show. "The topic? Oh—couples who have passed the six-month mark." Once you get there, they put you in a soundproof room. In the meantime, your best friend, who is about six months pregnant (she told you she was just bloated), and your boyfriend are on the stage talking about how they're screwing around, but you don't know it. And you're just smiling, 'cuz you can't hear and you're just happy to be on television. Furthermore, you think your man is going to propose to you with ten million people watching. Then you're escorted on the stage, and you're wondering why Tawanda is hugging on your man. And then, of course, you have to spread your dirty laundry to prove to the world that he is your man and he loves you and only you.

Have you noticed how the man is always sitting up there looking like he's got gas and never has anything to say, but maybe "Right. Right." Or "Naw. Naw. See it wasn't even like that." I swear that's all they have to say for themselves. And of course, the segment ends with Ricki asking, "Jutawn, what are you going to do?" The really stupid women will say something like, "He knows where his bread is buttered. He'll be back." Duh!

When I can bear to think about it, I am amazed at how stupid I have been in my relationships. Looking back, I realize it was pretty presumptuous of me to tell the last three guys I dated they were my soul mates. Or those couple of times I handed over my brain and let him navigate the relationship. "Whatever you think, honey."

What's the stupidest thing I've ever done for a man? Besides, of course, the time I believed my man when I caught him sucking on a woman's titties at a pool party, and he said he was teaching her the breast stroke. Let's just say, Dumbo wasn't just an elephant.

I have been very trusting in relationships. Okay, naive. Okay, just darn gullible! I confess I've made some mistakes which earned me many many stupid points, but thank God, I have learned.

Admit it, we've all done some dumb things to get or keep

a man. You told him you were pregnant knowing good and well that your river just flowed the night before. Or you quit your good job to follow him, but he didn't know quite where he was going. Doing a singularly dumb act and being repeatedly stupid are two totally different things. Women who sport that big "S" across their chests tend to be the ones who keep picking the same type of guys over and over, and think they're just having seven years of bad luck 'cuz they broke a mirror.

"How can I tell if I'm being stupid for a man?" you ask. First, if the last book you read was *The Little Engine that Could*, and you still haven't figured out why the chicken crossed the road, then there is probably little hope for you. For the rest of you, if you've experienced one of the following situations, you probably have been stupid for a man. Hey, but you bought this book, so that's a start.

Six Ways You Can Tell if You Are Stupid (for a Man)

1. You read in the paper that a third of all black men are in prison. You get yourself arrested so you can be with them.

2. Your man complains that you don't give him enough credit. You hand over your VISA and American Express cards.

3. You believe him when he says he's going to leave his wife.

4. Your man tells you he had a child during your two-year relationship. You wonder why you didn't experience labor pains.

5. You believe your man when he says he's been faithful, even though his penis is drooling like a newborn baby and you've mysteriously contracted a sexually transmitted disease.

6. Your man tells you he's a polygamist. You proclaim you're a Baptist, but not necessarily committed to it.

Bit O' Honey

Women who despise men fascinate me. I mean, I think every woman has her share of "How I Gave My All and That Man Did Me Wrong" stories. But bitter women let those experiences stick to them like flypaper. Women who celebrated after going to see *Waiting to Exhale* by setting their man's car on fire, missed the point of the movie. I think the purpose of the movie was to hold a mirror up to women and say, "See what we allow. . . . See what we put up with." For bitter women the movie was a confirmation of what they really think about men. "Men are no good. They cheat, lie, steal, do drugs, are gay, and will try to pick up another woman while I'm on my death bed." If you live by the creed "All Men Are Shit," I understand why you attract those bad apples.

I am proud of a lot of things in my life. I am proud of my family and friends. I'm proud of my work. I'm proud that I've kept my integrity in a business that sometimes applauds and rewards one for being less than honorable. And I am proud to say that I have felt the pain of relationships gone awry, but I'm working very hard not to come out a bitter woman. Oh, it has been tough too. Damn, is it tough! Over the years I have loved, thought I was in love, been told I was loved, fallen out of love, and been kicked in the ass by love. I know that it's a difficult battle.

I have been Florence Nightingale to men with medical (alcoholics), financial (broke), and mental (just plain crazy) problems. I step in, diagnose the situation, and prescribe what I feel is the best medicine—my love and devotion. Take a lot of both, and wake up with me in the morning.

I know that I am not perfect, but I have been careful not to bring any major baggage to any new relationship. I have never cheated. I am kind and sweet. And things go well—for a while, and then without fail, it happens. He asks for money. Oh, they don't really ask. They just simply imply. "Baby, you know my car is broke, I sure could use some . . . naw, never mind"; "Baby, I saw this fly apartment I want to move into, and I sure do wish I had the first and last months' rent . . . naw, forget it"; "Baby, could you give me . . . naw, I'm sorry I even said anything." And that was when I was a receptionist making $185 a week. Do I look like The National Bank of Kim? I must have IN KIM WE TRUST tattooed somewhere on my body in ink that's only visible to the male eye, because it *almost* always happens.

I know the questions you have milling around in your head. Kim, why do you feel the need to help these men? *Girl, I don't know.* What is it about you that attracts this type of man? *Girl, I just don't know.* Well, what are you going to do about it? *Girl, I'm trying to close down my savings and loan company!*

I am also trying to hold on to a Pollyanna-ish attitude, despite my bad luck with men. Somehow, I still believe that I can rise above it and keep my head to the sky. It's hard. Especially since my past history says that my relationships go down like the *Hindenburg.*

What I refuse to become is one of those real bitter bitches. You know the type: angry at all men, and it shows. She has that constant scowl on her face like the villains in those old black-and-white movies. She is closed emotionally and her heart is protected by a bulletproof vest. The irony is that bad relationships and bad men have made her this way. She can't find a man who will be good to her for the long haul and so now she hates them all. And what man would go near her now?

Save yourself, sistahs. When you feel that you are taking that turn onto Bitter Boulevard, pull over and remember the Bit O' Honey's Sad Tale:

Well, now, another sad story to tell.

The mother—— should go to hell.

I gave him love that was complete.

Bought him clothes to wear and food to eat.

I gave him sex every time he desired.

So much at times, my putang was on fire.

Now he says he wants some space.

Loves me no more, he said to my face.

He had found another and liked her charms.

And was going to live in her willing arms.

I cried and begged and beseeched him to stay.

And then he got up and walked away.

How could he have done this to me?

I vowed to gain revenge, you see.

Took his belongings to the garbage dump, and then

Told all his friends he had Herpes number ten.

Called him on the job till he got tired.

Called him so much he got fired.

That wasn't enough, my work was not done.

So I went out and bought myself a gun.

I'm doing twenty to life in a cold jail cell.

I don't think I handled this real well.

The moral of this verse if you don't know.

Is that it is better to just let things go.

Holding on to anger is bad, you see.

'Cuz they'll lock your ass up and throw away the key!

Desperado

When we were 18, my friends and I were very selective about the men we dreamed of dating. He had to be at least 6'2". He had to be smart, witty, articulate, ambitious, and come from a good family. He had to have an incredible smile and floss daily, be athletic, an excellent cook, a gentleman, considerate, polite, honest, respectful and caring, have knowledge of his African heritage, a sizable inheritance and an advanced degree, be studious, well-liked, and well-groomed. In addition, he had to treat his mother with respect, do community service work, be well traveled, believe in gun control, speak several languages, have no children, and never have been married.

Today, most of us have narrowed down that criteria quite a bit to—a man, preferably with a pulse.

It's true. As you get older, you're not as discriminating. You are more tolerant . . . more open-minded. For instance, I've had girlfriends who swore up and down they would never date men with kids. Five years later them kids are calling them stepmommy. Another one of my girlfriends swore she would never marry a broke man. When it came to finding a job, her husband was unluckier than a black man trying to catch a cab at night. But if you ask her about it now, she says, "Oh, girl, he's just a little financially challenged right now. He'll get on his feet. It's hard for a black man these days. What am I gonna do? Turn him away in the streets? I love him."

The older you get the more lax your standards become. Your thoughts become very practical. "He doesn't look that bad, and besides, that's why they invented the off position on a light switch."

So when does being more tolerant cross the line and become desperation? Elizabeth Taylor crossed the line about six husbands ago. If your biological clock is as big as the timepiece Flava Flav wears around his neck, I think you might have crossed that line. And if you're still waiting by the phone for him to call and it's been six months, you're so far gone, Flo-Jo couldn't catch you.

One reason desperation is so unattractive is because the person can be so obvious. If you want to know where the relationship is going by the end of the first date, that's not cool.

A desperate woman comes in handy when men just want to get their rocks off without a lot of red tape. She's like a credit card: easy to use, you can keep her in your back pocket, and she accepts anything you give her. A man who has any scruples doesn't have respect for a woman who is always available and agreeable and will do anything to be with him. Men like a challenge. If you're a woman who hands yourself to a man on a silver platter, you might want to think about how that looks.

"Yeah, that's easy to say, Kim. But I'm pushing thirty-five and I'm not married. Shoot, I want some kids."

Hell, adopt. Keep your nephews and nieces for a whole summer, become a childcare worker, go to a sperm bank, get a puppy. You have many options open to you. And believe me, all of those things are a lot more interesting than waiting on a man to throw a bone your way 'cuz he knows you're standing by to catch it.

The Funnel of Love

ages 18–22 I have a lot of energy. I'm optimistic about my future. My breasts are perky. I'm legal! It's raining men. At the bars, in the dorm, in the frat house. Life is good. Why settle for Mr. Wonderful, when Mr. Everything might be just around the corner?

ages 23–26 College was fun. I even learned a thing or two. I found a job to help pay off those student loans. Too bad I couldn't find a husband too. Maybe I'll meet him at an after-work set. Maybe at church. Why am I trippin'? I still look good. Besides, I have my career to concentrate on.

ages 27–32 Eek! Where has the time gone? All my friends are married or on their way. Let's see, there's Darren from work. So what if he's my grandfather's age. I did say I liked mature men. Maybe I will pass this time.

ages 33–40 Mr. Somebody or Mr. Anybody, please! Does anyone know the number to the nearest sperm bank? Where are the men? In prison . . . gay . . . married . . . I just need one.

Let the Games Begin

The biggest complaint I hear from women about men is that they don't want to commit. I can't say that has been my experience. Most of the guys I meet want to latch on to me like a seatbelt. Now that I think about it, I did date a guy once who was a little reluctant to commit. As a matter of fact, he couldn't even say the word "commit." He could say "Compton," "computer," "community," even "committee."

Maybe men know something we don't . . . naw, not possible. Maybe men are just very selective . . . okay, I'm reaching.

Maybe men are fearful that if they make a commitment, over time the relationship will become stale, causing the excitement and attraction they once had for us to slowly dissipate . . . am I getting warmer?

When you do find a man who is willing to commit, it's a whole new ball game. That dating and "getting to know you" stuff was child's play. You're in a *relationship* now. It's time to let your hair down, or take it off, as the case may be. It's time for him to *really* get to know you. You know, like when you were dating and you told him you weren't the jealous type, but you forgot to finish the sentence. "As long as an attractive woman is nowhere in the room." Or he told you he loved small breasts, but he meant on a chicken. Well, now it's time to deal with those insecurities and hang-ups.

I know what you're thinking. "Why does a relationship have to be like those damn Rubik's Cubes?" Remember those? Once you finally get all the colors lined up, you realize it wasn't worth the effort and aggravation. But the sense of accomplishment makes it worth it. Doesn't it?

Oh sure, the first six months are always fun because it's new. And the three months when you're dating before the six months, you're really window shopping. But once you get him home and rip off that clear plastic and take him out of the box, he doesn't seem to be life-size, like on the commercials. Or she doesn't do all the things she advertised she did. There's that annoying way he leaves his clothes lying around like he's a stripper. Or the way you constantly compare him to your ex-boyfriend like your ex is just away on hiatus. Or you find out your GI Joe comes already equipped with kids. Now that's a tough one.

I was in a relationship with this guy, Marcus, who had a two-year-old daughter. No matter what I did to try to be her friend, she wasn't having it. Everytime I was around her father, she would give me that look that Celie gave Mister in *The Color Purple.* Then she would point at me and say, "No!" I also found myself being jealous of the little girl. Marcus and I would get into arguments about it: "How come you never feed *my* food to me? . . Uh uh . . . she kicked me first . . . I thought you knew she was playing out in the street." I went from wanting to be this kid's stepmother to just wanting to step away from her altogether. I tried to look at the bright side. I mean, in 16 years Marcus and I could finally be alone together. But I'm certain I would have tried to strangle the devil-child before then.

Well, that's the risk you take when you're in a relationship with someone who has baggage—I mean children. Although being with a man who has kids can also be a positive. For one, it lets you see what type of father he is, just in case you want your own children with the man down the line. It's not a good sign if he's the type of guy who never sees his kids and when you ask him about it, he says, "I want to wait until they get older, 'cuz right now they're too young to understand who I am."

Regardless if there are children or meddling friends in the picture, a good relationship takes work, a lot of understanding, and patience. And you have to be ready to handle any and all situations that come into play. It's tough.

I sometimes wonder, if the government regulated relationships would we be much better off? (Yeah right, look what they did with cheese.) The way it would operate is once a couple decided they wanted to start a new relationship they would go down to the Department of New Relationships. It would be located somewhere in City Hall. Maybe next to the Public Records department or divorce court.

After completing an extensive survey on your expectations, you would sit down with a counselor to discuss your answers. Next, you would watch a short film on how to have a successful relationship. Then, once you've completed your physical and HIV test, you'd each be given a kit with all the necessary items to ensure a successful relationship: a bar of soap, toothbrush, perfume/cologne, nice lingerie/fresh pair of boxer shorts, a calendar with the dates of your anniversary and her birthday circled for him, and a box of tissue and a bottle of aspirin for those "Not tonight, I have a headache" nights, for her. And finally, you're given a list of rules and regulations you have to abide by while in the relationship. For example, "You will not take her for granted," and "You will not complain when he wants to watch six days of sports in a row."

You get your license in the mail six weeks later and a caseworker makes periodic home visits to see how you're doing.

I'm serious about this. The people in Washington mapped out the plans for the Department of New Relationships a long time ago. My informant tells me the plans somehow got misplaced. However, they recently turned up in the White House's library, along with a monkey wrench . . . with Colonel Mustard.

What Game Are You Playing?   ♥

Newlywed Game	**We all like this game because it's fun and exciting. You're in love and all is right with the world. You have your rose-colored glasses on, but you still think you can see clearly. The rain is gone. Birds are chirping. There's a rainbow in the sky. The future is bright.**
Red Light, Green Light	**You want to be his woman, then you don't. You want him to move in, but you just want to be friends. Make up your mind.**

Wheel of Fortune	The more time you spend together the more you uncover about each other. Most of the time he can guess what you're thinking without having to buy a vowel. And sometimes, to your *puzzlement*, no matter what's revealed, you can't read him.
Scrabble	We all know that communication is the key to a successful relationship, so if you've tried and he still doesn't seem to be listening, SPELL IT OUT for him.
Mousetrap	Over time a relationship can become stale. To keep from feeling like a caged animal with no hope of parole, be sure to keep the fires burning by doing something special every now and then. Be spontaneous! Write him a poem. Call her and tell her you love her.
Hide & Go Seek	I had a boyfriend who once told me he was working undercover and that I wouldn't be able to contact him for long periods of time. He must have thought I was a fool. If you spend more time playing detective trying to find your man than spending time with him, he may be trying to tell you something.
Jeopardy	"Who do you think is sexier, me or Halle Berry?" Be careful. Your response could put your relationship in serious turmoil. Does she want you to tell her the truth? Your best bet is to say your answer in the form of a question and hope it's the right one . . . "You?"

Operation	**Do you have those days when you just don't want to be bothered? Anything that comes out of his mouth makes you mad. He picks up on the hint so he becomes very careful around you, knowing if he touches you, you'll go off.**
Family Feud	**Some people can't help themselves, they have to involve their family in their relationship. "My mother said you should treat me like the precious gem that I am. My father said you should stop having your friends over to the house all of the time." And then she wonders why your parents don't like you. Survey says what goes on in your relationship should be between you and him.**
Solitaire	**Maybe you're better off alone. Maybe you realize you don't need the drama. Maybe he's caused you too much pain. The bottom line is you're alone and you can't seem to win.**

$\mathcal{P}$op that Question

Some of my single girlfriends and I had a powwow the other day. The topic: relationships. Lori had been dating the same guy for three years. She really loved him and by all indications, he seemed to love her. They had the same weird sense of humor; they were best friends; they took trips together; and they had a great sex life. "So what the problem is?" as my Uncle Bubba would say. They were at an impasse in their relationship. She was ready to take the relationship to the next level, and he pretty much liked the view from where they were.

Lori came to us because we were her girls, and she valued our opinions.

"Give him an ultimatum. If he can't see how rich he is with you in his life, then kick him to the curb and let him experience a little poverty. Life's too short, girlfriend," Dorothy offered.

"Well, I don't know. If he's good to you and he doesn't want to be with anybody else, I say just slow your roll. Give him time. Don't pressure him, let him come around in his own time," Jackie suggested.

"What you need to do is learn how to cook. Don't no man want to marry somebody who can't find their way around the kitchen. Both my ex-husbands told me that's why they married me," Laura boasted.

"Make him jealous. Start dating other men. It's not wise to put all your eggs in one kente cloth, anyway," Roslyn advised.

"Hell, trap that rat! Get pregnant, that'll make him marry you!" Sonya exclaimed.

"Naw, go on a pussy strike," added Arletha.

"Yeah, and if he don't want to wed, don't give him head," Toni, the poet, interjected.

Lori would have done better calling up Dionne's psychic friends. Then they all turned and looked at me like I stole something. "What do you think, Kim?"

Mama said there'd be days like this, I thought to myself. "Well, while you ladies have provided some excellent suggestions, I think Lori should follow her own heart and do what's best for Lori."

"That's dumb!" they chimed in.

"Yeah, but do any of you got a book deal?" I wanted to say. I later realized that my advice was probably dumb, but I thought it was better than what I was going to say, which was, "I don't know!"

That's a tough situation to be in. I'm sure a lot of women

have come to that fork in the road. It's like that one game on "The Price Is Right." The one that you have to decide whether to keep playing for the car or to stop and go home with the grandfather clock, sofa bed, and microwave you've already won. You can't make out what the audience is telling you to do. And all that you know is if you go on and play for the car and guess wrong, you lose it all. It's not fair. It's not fair that we can't get what we want, when we want it.

And the truth of the matter is, every man and situation are different. Dorothy's suggestion of giving him an ultimatum might work for one man, but it doesn't mean it's going to work with another. I had a friend who told her man that either he marry her or she was packing her bags and going back to Indiana. He called her bluff and told her *hasta la vista*. She left town quicker than Mark Fuhrman after he testified at the O.J. trial. And sure enough, three weeks passed and he was like, "Baby, come back." The man proposed. They were married within months and now they are very happy.

I had another friend who tried that and the week after she left, the man married another woman. So you never can predict these things. Instead of giving him an ultimatum, I think you need to give yourself one and decide whether you can be with the man and not be married to him.

And while Arletha's idea of withholding sex might put a little something on his mind, I don't think a pussy strike works when it comes to trying to get a man to marry you, for three reasons. One: pussy strikes aren't good for the economy. It just makes the "cock" holders angry and it brings down morale. It breeds an Us versus Them mentality. Two, you run into the problem of replacement workers. The skanks will be trying to cross the picket line as soon as they hear the news that your man hasn't been serviced. And three, if sexual intercourse is a normal part of your relationship, and it's something I'm assuming you enjoy, if you shut down the factory, you are going to be miserable too! And just think how you would feel if your man turned the tables on you and went on a penis strike. Yeah, you could probably last a little longer, but eventually you'd get as horny as Little Richard in the Dallas Cowboys' locker room.

With Sonya's bright idea about getting pregnant, you can be guaranteed of one thing: In nine months you're going to have a baby. There's nothing in the rule books that says baby = marriage. Sure, it will get his attention and it may even hurry him along, but men aren't like the men of the past. The concept of making an honest woman out of you doesn't compute anymore. When my friend sat her boyfriend down and gave him the news that they were going to have a baby, he was excited and nervous of course. But his first question was, "I guess that means we're going to be seeing a lot more of each other, huh?"

I once took Laura's advice. She swears the way to a man's heart was through his stomach. I was obsessed with this man and I wanted to marry him. I lived and breathed the cable cooking channel for months. I went out and bought all kinds of cookbooks, cooking utensils, aprons. I baked pies, casseroles, soufflés, you name it. I sampled everything I baked, gained 20 pounds, and he left me. So much for going the Betty Crocker route.

People ask me how did I get my ex-husband to propose and to be honest with you, I didn't do anything. It just so happened that we were both young and in love and he asked, and I accepted.

"Look, after the third week of the relationship, if everything is going good, I just tell them straight up that I need to know where things are going. I don't want them thinking, 'Why buy the cow when I'm getting the milk free?' 'Cuz I ain't trying to be no rented cow." That was my girlfriend's take on it. At press time she was still single.

Here's a thought. Instead of waiting for him, beat him to the punch and ask him first. Hey, this is the nineties, damn near a whole new century, so you have zero to lose. Or you can do what my lawyer friend Carol did. After dating Cedric for four years, she just started making preparations for her wedding. She set the date, booked the church, and consulted the preacher. Four months before the blessed event she began slowly letting Cedric in on her plans. "Cedric, aren't these wedding invitations nice?" Two weeks later, "Do you like these colors for bridesmaid dresses?" And then when out shopping one day, "This is the ring I want." Then, "Who is your best man going to be?" And finally, "Don't forget to pick up your tux."

During the wedding ceremony, when it came time for Cedric to say "I do," he got down on bended knee and asked, "Will you marry me?" The whole church burst out laughing. He eventually recovered and the family explained later that he was just a little nervous. Cedric realized some time later that something foul had occurred. He woke up in a cold sweat and turned to his wife of eight years and said, "I never asked you to marry me!" Carol rolled over and said simply, "The question is moot." Cedric went back to sleep.

The Other Woman

For any woman who marries a man, she is bound to come face to face with the other woman. It's unavoidable. I don't know what it is with men and their need to have these women in their lives to the extent that they do.

I remember the day my husband brought her into our home. We stood face to face and circled each other like two animals in a cage. She was older than I expected. I don't think she expected me to be as pretty as I was. I offered her something to drink. She declined. Then she came right to the point. "I know him better than you will ever know him. Don't ever forget that."

I countered with, "But I can give him something you will never be able to give him. And don't you forget that." She smiled coolly, grabbed her coat, and left.

I was happy that I had maintained my dignity. But, as I looked out the window, I saw my husband open the taxi door for her. I watched as he hugged and kissed her good-bye. At that moment, I realized that I had only won the battle. For he would go to her on that dreaded Sunday in May and she would be back for Christmas, and there wasn't a damn thing I could do about it because after all, she was his mother.

There is something to be said for a man and his mama. Show me a man who doesn't love his mother, and I'll show you a man who thinks *Showgirls* should have won Best Picture. A man can be the coolest brother around, then when he gets with his mother, he becomes as docile and gentle as a newborn lamb. I guess it's the womb connection or something because they behave like little boys.

And women, even if they don't want to admit it, get jealous, even if it's on a subconscious level. It doesn't matter how sweet or lovable she is to you, and it doesn't matter how secure you are in your relationship with your man. To a certain extent she's the competition. He compares you to her even when he doesn't mean to.

He reminisces about what a great cook, seamstress, caregiver, floral designer, housekeeper, and aviation pilot she was. How she made each day of his existence more special than the next. I mean, how can you top that? It's like she's the Cosby mom with a cape.

I never thought I would have those types of feelings toward my ex–mother-in-law until I noticed my husband doing something that gave me reason to feel this way. Every holiday, or if it was his mother's birthday, or if she was having her bunions removed, he would always send her a bouquet of flowers. I mean, really beautiful flowers. And that was great, but when I complained to him that I would also like to receive some flowers once in a while, he explained it to me simply this way: "She's my mother." And what was I, pig intestines?

Is Marriage All That?

Okay, so he finally proposed (while you weren't having sex) and he didn't send an impostor to the church in his place. You can now proclaim as loudly and proudly as Margaret Avery's character, Shug, did in *The Color Purple*, "I's married now!" So did you do the right thing? Are you being "till death do us smart"? Have you been bamboozled, hoodwinked? Did Plymouth Rock land on you?

I have mixed feelings about the whole marriage thing. On one hand, I feel like it's an archaic custom that played out a long time ago. Roles today are interchangeable. I was at the store the other day looking for a box wrench for a project I was doing around the house. So I asked a man next to me for help. He turned to his wife and asked, "Honey, is this a box wrench?" She went on to explain to me that I had in my hand an open wrench, and then pointed me to what I needed. It blew me away. And I thought about how I didn't fit the traditional wife role when I was married, either. I wasn't very domestic. I'd wash a dish every now and then. It just seemed easier to throw out the dirty dishes and buy new ones. Then I discovered paper plates.

I mean, years ago, marriage wasn't just about love and commitment. It was more of a business arrangement. It still is in many cultures. Women provided the children and men . . . provided. Taking a bride was also about men acquiring property. That's why the father had to pay a dowry and why the woman took her husband's name. I guess that hasn't changed all that much today. Except now it's all about the woman acquiring property after she divorces.

On the other hand, I think if two people are really sincere, marriage is a courageous and loving act that says to the world, "I have found the person I want to share my morning breath with for the rest of my life."

These days I think people put more emphasis on the wedding day than the forty or fifty years that are supposed to come afterward. I mean, how did it go from a simple jump over a broom to a full-fledged production extravaganza? My wedding day was very simple. We spent approximately twelve dollars. Two dollars for the subway, five bucks for a plastic bouquet of flowers, and four bucks for a couple of pretzels and sodas. And badda boom badda bing, we were married.

A couple of years ago, I got a wedding invitation that read, "Mr. and Mrs. So and So invite you to the Biggest Wedding of the Century. Starring our daughter, So and So, and the groom-to-be, So and So. Star-studded reception immediately following." I felt like I was going to the Emmys. They had a Charles and Di wedding and ended up just like Charles and Di.

There is a story going around about this woman who had a lavish church wedding planned: exquisite flowers, twenty bridesmaids, a huge wedding cake, and a Barbados honeymoon planned and paid for by her parents. She was a beautiful bride in her Valentino gown with a 20-foot train. I mean the day was like a fairy tale until the groom stood up at the reception to toast his new bride. He said, "To my lovely bride and to my best man. I am giving you the tickets to Barbados where we were supposed to go on our honeymoon since you have been sleeping together behind my back for the last three months. Enjoy." And then he and his parents walked out, leaving the bride, the best man, and the guests stunned beyond disbelief. Now, of course she was embarrassed as all hell, but she had just had the wedding of her dreams. They got an annulment the next day and she went to Barbados with the best man. I mean, what's wrong with this picture?

Sometimes, I think, if two people are destined to be together why should you have to go through this whole ritual thing? Marriage is in the heart. That's what one of my friends told this woman he was with to get her mind off of marriage.

By no means do I want to discourage people who want to do so from having a big hoedown of a wedding. I just want you to realize the memory of that day won't be as special if three years, or even fifteen minutes, down the line you realize you married a monster.

My friend Victor used to complain that months after he got married, his wife was invaded by body snatchers. She treated sex like a distant cousin, and she was beginning to look like Nell Carter around the middle. He said he wanted a divorce on the grounds of false advertising. Some people view marriage not as a special bond between two equally yoked people, but merely as a race that ends when he says, "I do." And before you know it, he's saying, "On your mark, get set . . . let's part!" Don't let pressure or somebody else's agenda push you down the aisle.

Believe me, what you did to "get" him, you damn sure have to keep doing to keep him. The trouble is, because you were in such a rush to "get" him, you forgot to get to know him and maybe you've discovered you don't like what you forgot to get to know. Then what? It's too late to throw him back. Divorce him. That's simple, right? Well, maybe he's a little possessive. After all, there is the one that got away and the one that wouldn't leave—and maybe that's him. Now what? You fake your own death. Move to another part of the country, change your identity, and give up all communications with your friends and family. It could happen.

Now sometimes men change after marriage too. After a year of marriage, my friend Theresa began sleeping in a separate room from her husband. His snoring had gotten out of control. "You had to know about his problem before you decided to marry him," I insisted.

"No, actually his doctor says the entire time we were dating, he had subconsciously held his breath when he slept with me because he knew it would present a problem in our marriage. The doctors are saying it's a medical miracle!"

I say the wedding bells were ringing so loudly in her ears she ignored the snoring. Now that's a miracle.

As for my own marriage, let's just say it didn't work out. I will say we were really young when we did it but all the love in the world sometimes can't stop two people from growing up or away from each other. We were emotionally married for five years and legally married for ten. (He kept refusing to agree to a divorce. What can I say, I am irresistible). Now that's my story, and I'm stickin' to it. I will always love and respect the brother and I'm happy to say we remain friends to this day.

At this point in my life, I really don't know if I will ever marry again. I'm becoming "set in my ways." I don't know why, but the weirdest things bother me. For instance, I absolutely hate when guys come in from outdoors and don't wash their hands before rubbing all over my body. That just irritates me to no end. But, I don't mind squeezing pimples and digging for ear wax. My own or anybody else's. It makes me cringe when I see finger or hand prints all over a car's window, but I don't mind if the car is dusty. Go figure. And whistling and gum cracking are forbidden, unless I'm doing it, of course. I'm not selfish, I'm just used to living alone now and I've had time to think about what's important to me.

So I let men I'm interested in know that I'm free, but it'll cost them. And I'm not talking financially. Though I would just once like to date a man whose wardrobe consists of more than a damn barrel. The good news is that I don't want a man to dig deep into his pockets. I want him to dig deep into his heart. I want his love, his devotion, and loyalty. So it's going to cost him emotionally and spiritually. I'm ready to love again. And the man who is going to love me back is going to have to pay the price. My love is like having stock in a solid company.

171

You buy shares cautiously because you're not looking for any quick returns. You have a long-term investment plan. If you pay close attention to the market, with time you'll have a better sense of your stock's performance. By risking, over time, the dividends you'll reap will be worth it.

♥

Livin' Single

I sometimes wonder if love is a temporary emotion. It lasts for about six months and then it becomes tolerance. Why else would you stay in a relationship with someone who is no good for you? That's like eating a gallon of Häagen-Dazs when you know you're lactose intolerant. Or eating a box of prunes right before you run a marathon. Talk about the runs! You want to get married and have a slew of kids, but he isn't interested in tying the knot and he is not interested in having children due to the fact that he was raised by wolves. You knew this from jump, but you thought you could do a David Copperfield on his ass and change him into Bill Cosby. Or she tells you she loves you like a brother, but you wear her down until she agrees to be your woman, knowing in time she'll learn to love you. And by the time you put all this effort into turning this person into someone they are not, they have kind of grown on you like toe jam. And then you realize ending the relationship is as painful as finding out you owe the Internal Revenue Service $20,000 because of a technicality.

Stop the Relationship, I Want to Get Out

It's really hard, especially if you loved that person and gave the relationship your all. If you just had lukewarm feelings about the guy, it's like getting one of those tetanus shots. It might sting for a quick second, but soon you're over it and wondering what all the fuss was about. When you really really love a person, and for some reason or another it doesn't work out, then that's the worst feeling in the world. All the times in my life when I was growing up and found myself in serious pain don't compare to the pain I feel when I have a broken heart. The time when I slid into a concrete home plate and scraped all the skin off my knee where you could see clear to my knee bone, and blood was gushing everywhere and the other kids were running away like they stole something—it hurts worse than that. Or that time when I accidentally poked myself in the eye with a razor-sharp eye pencil.

Tolerance hurts. It's like an addiction, and once you both agree to break up and he's got all his ratty drawers out of your house, that's when you start going through withdrawal. The withdrawal period can last anywhere from three months to a decade. And if you're like me you cry, you eat, and cry some more. Excuse me a minute while I cry some more. . . . You think about calling. You dial the number in your head. You pick up the phone. You call your girlfriend instead and tell her you miss him and want to call. She tells you all the great reasons why you shouldn't. You flip through your *Essence* magazine, which reinforces your girlfriend's advice. You call him anyway. And most of the time you don't regret it because it gave you the fix you needed to get through the night. It brings you comfort that he was at home and he sounded as miserable as you did.

If it's a bad break-up and you didn't initiate it, it's even more difficult. You go through stages and of course, denial is always the first stage. "He'll be back. Just watch. He'll call and ask me to take him back." The next thing you know you're checking with the phone company to make sure your phone is working properly. Then you get pissed. And you're angrier than Mr. T at a jewelry convention that has only silver. You're pissed at yourself because you've gone and done it again. You opened up your heart, only to have this man who must have been posing as a heart specialist come steal it for some transplant operation. You're pissed at all the wasted time. It's like spending months on a term paper and having your professor give you a check mark instead of a letter grade. Then you get depressed because your score card has more strikes than hits and while your grades for career and community service might be A−, you feel like you're getting a big fat F in love. And then you start feeling guilty. You think maybe it was your fault or maybe you could have tried harder, been more patient, been less demanding. Then the final phase is pure loneliness. Lonely like how the Unabomber must have felt in that cabin all by himself. Because after a while you get used to having a person around, even if you fought, got on each other's nerves, and he was just okay in bed. Mediocrity isn't a crime.

And then the phases start all over again: denial, angst, depression, guilt, loneliness. And once you've succeeded through the withdrawal period, and he hasn't called so you call him and he's moved on with his life, and you can tell from talking to him that you're nowhere in the picture, eventually you realize it was probably for the best.

Then you vow to never fall in love again. But just the way the rinse cycle happens before you know it, six months later you find soul mate #22. Women have this inexplicable capacity to love a man with every fiber of their being, and in so doing have the capacity to feel the deep sense of pain that is caused when he decides to step. A man's capacity for such love is rare, to my knowledge. We women also have the ability to forgive and forget. We usually move on to the next relationship, sometimes cautiously, but always, always willing to give 100 percent. Men, on the other hand, never forgive themselves if a woman makes a combination platter out of his heart. A bout with heartbreak renders him speechless most times, and at best, ambivalent toward any future relationships.

To properly bury our dead relationships when they end, it is important to ask ourselves what we learned from the experience. I know what some of you are saying: "I learned he obviously wasn't the one!" Contrary to what Elizabeth Taylor or Whoopi may tell you, it's not healthy to jump in and out of relationships.

I learned after the first couple of heartbreaks that you should try not to seek comfort from friends because you get those stale comments that have been around so long they sometimes get taken out of context. "Don't worry about it, girl. Yes, there is a wound, but since you have nothing but time now, go buy you some heels and it'll be all right."

"I think you mean 'time heals all wounds.' "

"Whatever."

Or, "Well, you know what they say. If he's absent, to hell with him and the fonder you can grow."

"I think that's 'absence makes the heart grow fonder.' And that really doesn't help me one bit."

So I've learned how to keep my pain to myself.

Ten Ways to Tell if You Should End Your Relationship

1. You need an arbitrator to determine who gets first dibs on the bathroom.

2. You remind him of your mother.

3. You start to enjoy your fake orgasm.

4. It has become difficult to talk to each other—about the weather.

5. Lately when he dreams of you, you're always in a coffin.

6. You use his picture to line your bird cage.

7. You leave the cap off the toothpaste to make him mad, even though you hate it too.

8. You'd rather open your door to a Jehovah's Witness than have sex.

9. You lick and mail all of his rare stamps from his prized collection.

10. You hate each other.

A Pigeon Trying to Cross the Street

The other day I was driving down the street and I saw the strangest thing (I mean besides Reverend Al Sharpton with an afro). As I sat there waiting for the traffic light to turn green, I saw a pigeon at the crosswalk trying to walk across the street. No pigeon shit. True story. Every time it would attempt to walk across the street, the pigeon would rush back to the curb, realizing the danger of the passing cars. "You can fly, you stupid pigeon!" I wanted to scream. But the pigeon stood dumbfounded, going back and forth like a wind-up toy trying to get across that street. Then I thought maybe momma and daddy pigeon forgot to tell baby pigeon she had wings. Maybe daddy pigeon was too busy working, trying to support the family, and momma pigeon was too busy feeding and cooking and cleaning, and trying to get by, that it hadn't occurred to her that she hadn't let her baby know that she had wings. They didn't tell her that she might not be able to soar through the air like a great eagle, but she could use her wings, at the very least, to get across a busy intersection.

Sometimes I think that's what happens to a lot of sistahs

as little girls. We're told that we can't do something because we're not pretty enough or smart enough, or sometimes we're not told anything at all. Or we're told we need a man to make us whole. That a man is the key to your ignition, the missing jigsaw piece to the puzzle, the bread for your toaster, the happily ever after to your fairy tale. That's what we are told, right? If this is true, then how will we ever know what we are capable of?

While getting my hair braided the other day, I was sitting and thinking (it takes 15 hours, so I had plenty of time), how boys were the center of my life all while I was growing up. I spent most of my adolescence thinking about boys. Thinking about the ones I thought were cute. Knowing that if they spoke to me, how it would make my day. I can remember when I was ten going through the Sears catalog picking out furniture and baby clothes for my future. I would add the stuff up and get so frustrated because I would think, man, my husband is going to have to be making big bank to support us.

Some of us stay in relationships that are not good for us because we don't think we can find anyone better. Some of us are just like that poor pigeon who doesn't know she can fly. How sad. That's as deep as I'm going to get.

Single Sistah's Bedtime Prayer

Now I lay me down to sleep.

Please don't send me no more creeps.

Please just send me one good man

One without a wedding band.

One good man who's sweet as pie

Who brushes his teeth and doesn't lie.

Livin' Single

Who dresses neat and doesn't smell

And is sexy like my man Denzel

Is super-rich like Michael J.

On second thought, that's okay.

Man, if I should die before I wake

That would truly take the cake;

No matrimony or honeymoon.

No fancy reception planned for June.

No throwing of the wedding bouquet.

Please, God, don't let me go out that way.

If I die before I meet Mr. Right

I won't go out without a fight.

But then again with my dumb luck,

He'd probably be just some schmuck.

The single life is not that bad

I know it's just a passing fad.

I won't be blue. I will not frown.

Besides, I like my toilet seat down.

No more makeup, won't comb my hair.

So never mind this stupid prayer

The single life will do just fine.

So what's up, girlfriend? It's party time!

Get your TV Guide and coffee cup.

Let's talk about Fox's Thursday line-up.

At 8:30 is "Living Single."

Hand me the Lay's not them damn Pringles.

I love Khadijah, that's my girl.

And Synclaire is like a little pearl.

A little naive, but that's okay.

She's Obie's honey 24/7 and a day.

Regine, a diva from the start

Has a wig for every single part.

In the meantime where's Max and Kyle

Probably getting busy on the bathroom tile.

Those girls make single life seem real cool.

Maybe I'll go back to school.

Get a Ph.D. in singlehood.

Write a book, get paid, it's all good!

Sistah to Sistah

How could I write a book about dating without at least trying to explore loving sexual relationships between women? Let's be real. Lesbianism is alive and lickin'. Oops, I think I meant kickin'! I never understood why some people are so opposed to the whole concept of homsexuality and bisexuality. And let's stop talking about people who date people of their same gender like they're from another planet or something. I remember one time I went shopping with a girlfriend and she saw this woman she knew. She turned to me as the woman was approaching us, and whispered, "She's bi." When the woman approached us, I said, "Hi, Bi. I'm Kim." And my friend and the woman had the strangest looks on their faces. "I'm going to go look at those clothes. Bye, Bi. It was really nice meeting you."

I mean, as a woman, I think we should be able to relate, or at least have the capacity to empathize with one another. I hear what some of you are saying already. "Ain't nothing another woman can do for me. If it ain't no dick, then that's just sick." Well, I think people should feel free to love whomever they want to love. If it's natural for you, I say go for it. But please be honest with yourself.

I don't have a problem with women loving women, I have a problem with women loving women because they really *hate* men. I wonder if you were to take a census of the lesbian population what would you find? You would probably find some women who are biologically born with a predisposition to be attracted to women. Then there are those who are just bored and want to try something trendy. "Oh, no, I'm not gay, I have a boyfriend. I just thought it would be fun to rub on somebody's titty. That's the new in thing." And the rest would be bitter, disillusioned women who have been messed over by men and prefer the company of other womankind. It is not hard to spot them. They are partial to lumberjack shirts, mustaches, comfortable shoes, and k.d. lang. Just kidding. I'm a comedian. Now a gang of lesbians is going to tie me down and lick me to death. Hmmm, intriguing isn't it? But I digress. While I don't have a problem with the gay lifestyle, I personally couldn't get into it because I'm attracted to men. I believe that a penis has to be somewhere in the room during sex for me to get off, but hey, that's what strap-ons are for. As much hatred and craziness that's out there, I'm for any kind of anything that's loving.

If you really want to have fun while you're going through your drought, go out and find yourself a gay male friend. Usually gay men love you unconditionally, are sensitive, have great taste in fashion, and will give you amazing decorating tips. Go ahead, try to find a straight decorator. They usually have compassion that rises above sexuality, and love fabulous black female divas: Diana Ross, Donna Summer, Kim Coles—actually I am a D. I. T (diva in training). I know, I know, you're going to say I am stereotyping, but I speak from very personal experience. First of all, I live in West Hollywood, a neighborhood in L.A. nick-named Boystown. And if I want to see some of the most beau-tiful, well-kept bodies, honey, I just go to the supermarket or the local gym. Secondly, I volunteer with several gay- or AIDS-related charities, and lastly, one of my very best friends is a gay, thirty-something, Jewish man. We love each other so much that I call him my gay Jewish husband. He acts like my husband sometimes, being protective, loving, and oh, how he worries. Well maybe he is more like my mother. We have been through a lot together, almost coming to blows over cute guys in the market. ("I saw him." "No I saw him first.") We have been through each other's operations, my knee and his liposuction. I have to admit that my homo men have been around longer than some of my hetero ones. You haven't lived until you've gone out dancing with a bunch of boys. I am taking diva lessons from the best.

The Diary of a Single Sistah

January 1
Dear Journal,
I broke up with Stan at 11:59 p.m. Right before the ball dropped in Times Square. Out with the old, poor, broke

loser, and hopefully a new love will come into my life this
year. So far this has been a good year for me. I've made a
list of my resolutions, and at the top is to find my soul
mate. He's out there. I know he is.

January 12
Dear Journal,
I met this guy, Raymond, at my new gynecologist's office.
He was my new gynecologist. The good news is, if it works
out, he'll probably know me better than I know myself. The
bad news is, he'll probably know me better than I know
myself. I might invite him to my friend Monica's wedding.
We'll see.

January 31
Dear Journal,
I found out by our third date why Raymond loves being a
gynecologist a little too much! Damn dog! Monica's
wedding was beautiful and her husband's best man was
attractive and available, and giving me the eye all night.
But of course, I was with Raydog at the time. I just got
off the phone with Monica to see if I could track the
brother down. She let me know the bad news. He hooked
up with one of the bridesmaids and they're shacking up as I
write.
Oh well.

February 14
Dear Journal,
Four women received flowers at work today. Two of them
received boxes of chocolates. And one went home sick. It
was me. I didn't want to be a witness to all the displays of
love and affection. Next year, I'll have a man to share my
Valentine's Day.

March 2
Dear Journal,
Today was a stinky day. I just laid around the house. I
didn't take a bath. As a matter of fact, I haven't let water
touch me. I unplugged the phone. Didn't even turn on the
tube. Instead, I put on some John Coltrane, meditated, and
basked in my stinkiness. I could get used to this single life
stuff. It's all right.

March 3
Dear Journal,
I met a man at the Department of Motor Vehicles. He is a
god. In the dictionary under tall, dark, and handsome is his
picture. His eyes were dark and sexy, and his mustache
spelled out my name when he smiled. I could tell he had
been intimate with a barbell by the way his well-formed
muscles pulsated from underneath his white, starched shirt.
And from his pearly whites I knew that his dentist didn't
ever have to remind him about his six-month visits. We're

going out tonight. Cross your bookmark, this might be the one!

April 1
Dear Journal,
Boy was I fooled. He told me on the first date, "If you treat me right, you just might become my number-one lady." I retorted, "If I treat you wrong, will you promise to scratch my name off the list and never call me again?" He was a jerk. I should have seen it coming. He wore eyeliner, for God's sake.

April 23
Dear Journal,
Another wedding. This time I got suckered into being a bridesmaid. Robin promises I'll be able to wear the dress again. Right. Where can I wear a green chiffon dress with double ruffles around the butt? Other than that, me and my girl Stacie sat around and watched videos all weekend. Exciting, right? It helps to have someone to share in your misery. Stacie is upbeat and funny. I like hanging out with her. Man, I just realized I haven't had sex in over a year. I wonder what Stacie would look like with a mustache.

May 13
Dear Journal,
Still single and no prospects.

June 11
Dear Journal,
Still single and no prospects.

July 31
Dear Journal,
Okay, this is getting ridiculous. The summer is damn near over and I am still manless. Maybe it's because I look like crap. You know what I'm going to do? I'm going to get a complete makeover. I'm going to shed some of these unwanted pounds, and I'm going to find my soul mate this year, no matter what.

September 13
Dear Journal,
Well, I got my first weave today. Now I know what those guys who belong to those men's hair clubs feel like! I'm losing the weight. My next goal is to get out more. Look out world, here I come.

November 3
Dear Journal,
Sorry I haven't written in a while. I've been too busy hanging out. They know me by name at the health club now. I joined a dating service! Can you believe it? So far I've been meeting a lot of nice guys. No one who floats my boat, but it's been interesting.

December 19
Dear Journal,
It finally happened! I found my soul mate. Now every morning, I get up and look at my true love in the mirror, and I can't help smiling at her. Maybe next year, I'll find my significant other. Right now I'm having too much fun with me!

Okay, so things didn't turn out quite how some of us planned it. Either the man of our dreams, who we promised to love and cherish, turned out to be the man of our nightmares, or the man of our dreams is still in our dreams and hasn't yet materialized into a real, live, breathing person. Yes, some days it's frustrating. Just once when that unwanted mutant slithers up to you and asks, "Hey, baby, are you married?" Just once you want to say, "Damn straight!" and shove that rock in his face. And some days you get tired of feeling like that spoiled kid from *Home Alone*. And when you're single and you're home all day alone, after a while you talk out loud, just because you haven't heard your own voice in so long. I do that. Don't you?

And yes, if you are single, you are more likely to be discriminated against. People look at you funny if you buy a Double Whopper, they laugh at you if you want to play double Dutch, they smirk if you're chewing Doublemint gum. The way this book was formatted is an obvious example of how discrimination against singles goes on every minute of every hour and we just look the other way. What am I talking about? This book is double spaced. See what I'm saying? That wasn't my wish. I was adamant about it being entirely single spaced to show how passionate and proud I am to be single, but because the couples are the ones in power, we have to live by their rules. It's a conspiracy, I tell you.

Despite the discrimination and the loneliness, like the express checkout line, the single life has its privileges. Or is that American Express? If you want to go to a movie, or a play or whatever, you have no restrictions, no one to compromise with. You go see what you want to see when you want to see it. Now I know what you're saying: "But I don't like going places by myself." Have you tried it? I have friends who have never been out to a movie or dinner alone because they say they think it would feel too weird. That's unfortunate because I think what they are really saying is they don't feel they could enjoy their own company.

I have to admit, the first time I went out alone to a movie, I was uneasy too. And it showed. An older couple saw me cowering at the ticket booth and insisted on buying my ticket because they felt bad for me. Another couple offered to buy me popcorn and Jujubees. I didn't end up spending a dime. Now after getting the hang of being "singled out," I don't look as pitiful anymore. People just give me the once over and say, "Oh, that's that girl from 'Living Single' out alone again." And a couple of times, I've met some single guys who also ventured out alone.

Another great thing about being single is if you want to be a slob, there is no one to stop you. I will never forget once when I didn't clean my place for months. I left open food containers out, dirty dishes piled to the ceiling, grimy clothes, magazines, and newspapers stacked high. I was comfortable, you know. There was no man around to tell me I was a filthy, disgusting pig. It felt good. Then I came home one day and a gang of roaches were outside my door protesting that it was too messy in there, even for them. That's when I decided it was time to tidy up a bit.

The point is this: For that brief moment, before the roach revolt, and before the fire department declared my place not fit for humans to live in, and before the subsequent eviction notice and criminal lawsuits and fines, I was happy not having to answer to a man about how I chose to live my life.

I have a girlfriend who feared she was going to be an old maid, so she married a man she didn't love. Now she's a divorced old maid. I believe it's all about your state of mind.

I remember one day feeling lonely and sorry for myself and I decided to do something about it. I went to a retirement center to volunteer my time. I never felt so at peace and loved than at that center. The people were so warm and they enjoyed the companionship. I was a little hurt when they said I couldn't move in, and I had to cut back my visits to two days a week when Edy, the 87-year-old woman on the fourth floor, said I was depressing her with my heartbreak hotel stories. She threatened to get a restraining order on me. I didn't take it personally. What is important is I got out and did something about my situation.

Oddly enough, during the course of writing this book, I met a wonderful guy, got engaged, started planning a wedding, and six months later, I got cold feet. And it was nothing he did, though like a detective on a fact-finding mission, I found things, excuses, like "Uh, honey, it's annoying when you do that thing. Could you stop it, please?"

"What's that, dear?"

"Could you please stop breathing?"

I thought by the time I got to the end of the book, I would have the answers to the meaning of life and love. Believe it or not I am just like you. My so-called "celebrity status" does not make it easier to find and keep love. But what I have learned is, the single life, like life, is really what you make of it. Yeah, being married and having children sounds wonderful and all that, but the bottom line is we must live in the present and make the most of that time.

Perhaps I'll never find Mr. Matrimony, or maybe like my manager Sinclair suggested, God is saving the best for last. Hey wait a minute—I think he stole that from Vanessa Williams.

A wise woman told me recently that if the worst thing that ever happened to her in her life is she never got married and never bore children, then she couldn't complain. That's an excellent point. While you're concentrating on what you don't have in your life, you miss out or lose sight of what you do have. Like good friends and your family, who have to love you and can't get rid of you, no matter what. And when those folks let you down or when you can't depend on them, go to the source. I'm talking about that place inside your heart and soul that says you are the most unique and wonderful person that you've had the opportunity to know.

And remember, depression is not a disease only for the single. Don't think marriage or being in a relationship is the cure-all and end all of loneliness or unhappiness. Search for the joy inside yourself, 'cuz it's there if you sit still and listen. So stop fighting and go with the flow. Maybe, just maybe, you'll discover you like yourself with or without a man. At that moment, you'll realize the true meaning of life and having done so, you'll drop to your knees, kiss this book, look toward the heavens and shout, "I'm living! I'm actually living single and loving it!"

Appendix:
The Dating Survey

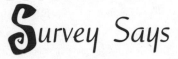

Survey Says

I sent surveys out to a cross-section of my friends and acquaintances because of my sincere interest in what people are looking for in a mate. Plus, I am nosy, uh uh, curious. In the name of science, I decided to report my findings to the general public. I enjoyed reading these responses so much that I just had to share them with you. As you will soon see, people love to talk! Now for your information, these were mailed out with self-addressed stamped envelopes so that they could be returned anonymously and on my dime, so people had no excuse. Also I did change some of the details to protect people's privacy. Good thing too, because I discovered after receiving almost 100 responses that most of the people who answered are freaks, weirdos, and sexual deviants. Birds of a feather, eh? I love them anyway. See the results beginning on page 207.

By the way, here are the actual surveys, one for women and one for men. If you'd like to join in the fun, I invite you to tear out the pages, fill in your answers, and drop them in the mail. I am going to do a subsequent book reporting the answers you send in. Use extra paper if necessary. I know you have a lot to say.

Send to: Kim Coles
             c/o Hyperion
             114 Fifth Avenue
             New York, NY 10011

Sistah Study

(Please feel free to expand on any of your answers. Be descriptive and as open as you like. Feel free to use the back or another sheet of paper if you need more space. You do not have to include your name. Please print, have fun, and thank you!)

1. *What do you look for in a mate? Please rate the following qualities in order of importance.*

    2 – Very important (as in FBI/CIA national-security kind of importance)

    1 = Important (as in Brink's armored truck kind of importance)

    0 = Not very important (as in a security guard at a mini mall kind of importance)

    _____ Intelligence (Can he get through a Dr. Seuss book without using a dictionary?)

    _____ Education (Did he stop at the third grade or does he have his doctorate from Harvard in the study of astrosocialphysism in aardvarks?)

    _____ Sense of humor (Do you like your man to be Silly like Sinbad, Electric like Eddie, or Stoic like Spike?)

    _____ Height (Kareem Abdul Jabbar or Emmanuel Lewis?)

    _____ Career (Does he have one?)

    _____ Morals (Does he have them; do you have them, for that matter?)

_____ Community activism (Is he a member of the neighborhood watch or do the neighbors need to be watching his ass?)

_____ Religion (Does he believe?)

_____ Hygiene (Does he wash his ass?)

_____ Financial Status (Rich Man, Poor Man, Indian Chief?)

_____ Penis Size (Does it really matter? *Hell yes,* but don't let me influence your answer)

_____ Fashion Sense (*GQ* or *Field and Stream?*)

2. *Which body type do you prefer?*

_____ The Incredible Hulk (muscle-bound hunk-o-rama)

_____ Slim Jim (Jimmy Walker type)

_____ Regular build (Not too big, not too small)

_____ Teddy Bear (cuddly)

_____ Big Poppa (Big Luther Vandross, Barry White, more-to-love type of man)

3. *Which skin color do you prefer?*

_____ Vanilla (white boy) _____ Cinnamon

_____ Vanilla with nuts (Italian)   _____ Mocha

_____ Coffee

_____ Butterscotch

_____ Dark Chocolate

_____ Caramel

_____ Licorice

199

4. *What kind of hair do you prefer on your man's head?*

_____ Dreadlocks   _____ Curly

_____ Straight   _____ Bald or balding
(with or without
toupee?)

5. *What kind of voice do you prefer?*

_____ Barry White—Bass

_____ Johnny Mathis—Tenor

_____ Michael Jackson—Serious Soprano

_____ Kermit—brother with a frog in his throat

6. *Are you in a relationship right now?*

_____ Yes _____ No
(if no, skip to question 8)

7. *What kind of relationship is it?*

_____ Committed

_____ Casual

_____ "I don't even like his ass, I'm just biding my
time."

8. *What was your last relationship like?*

    _____ Committed

    _____ Casual

    _____ "I didn't even like his ass, I was just biding my time."

9. *What was the cause of the break-up?*

10. *How often do you have sex? (list number of times)*

    _____ Every day (You lucky sonofabitch)

    _____ Every week

    _____ Every month

    _____ Never, I'm a virgin (You lying sonofabitch)

11. *How often do you orgasm?*

    _____ Every time (You lying sonofabitch)

    _____ Sometimes

    _____ Never (Maybe you should see a doctor)

12. Where is the strangest place you ever did "the nasty"?

13. What's your favorite position? (This has nothing to do with the book, I'm just a nosy sonofabitch)

14. Describe your dream man. Please be as descriptive as you can.

15. What was the worst date you ever had? Please be as descriptive as you can.

16. What was the best date you ever had? Please be as descriptive as you can.

Mr. Man Study

(Please feel free to expand on any of your answers. Be descriptive and as open as you like. Feel free to use the back or another sheet of paper if you need more space. You do not have to include your name. Please print, have fun, and thank you!)

1. *What do you look for in a mate? Please rate the following qualities in order of importance.*

   2 = Very important (as in FBI/CIA national-security kind of importance)

   1 = Important (as in Brink's armored truck kind of importance)

   0 = Not very important (as in a security guard at a mini mall kind of importance)

   _____ Intelligence (Can she get through a Dr. Seuss book without using a dictionary?)

   _____ Education (Did she stop at the third grade or does she have her doctorate from Harvard in the study of astrosocialphysism in aardvarks?)

   _____ Sense of humor (Do you like your woman to be Goofy as Gilda, Lovable like Lucy, or Crazy as Carol Burnett?)

   _____ Height (Amazon or Pygmy?)

   _____ Career (Does she have one?)

   _____ Morals (Does she have them, or do you mind that she's a "ho"?)

_____ Community activism (Is she a member of the neighborhood watch or do the neighbors need to be watching her ass?)

_____ Religion (Does she believe?)

_____ Hygiene (Does she wash her ass?)

_____ Financial Status (Rich Bitch or Welfare Queen?)

_____ Breast Size (Flat as a pancake or Dolly Parton?)

_____ Fashion Sense (Donna Karan or Kmart special?)

2. *Which body type do you prefer?*

_____ Big Mama (More to love, like Nell Carter or Delta Burke type)

_____ Regular build (Not too big, not too small)

_____ Long and Lean (Anorexic or Naomi Campbell)

_____ Little Bit (Petite like Jada Pinkett and Dr. Ruth)

3. *Which skin color do you prefer?*

_____ Vanilla (white girl)	_____ Cinnamon
_____ Vanilla with spice (Italian girl)	_____ Mocha
_____ Butterscotch	_____ Coffee
_____ Caramel	_____ Dark Chocolate
	_____ Licorice

4. What kind of hair do you prefer on your woman's head?

_____ Braids   _____ Curly

_____ Dreadlocks   _____ Weave

_____ Bone Straight   _____ Bald

5. How do you feel about a woman's past experiences? Do you prefer:

_____ a virgin (so I can mold her the way I want)

_____ Experienced (Been around enough to know what to do, but the muscle is still tight down there)

_____ Ho (I want her fast ass to teach me a few things)

6. Describe your favorite body part. (e.g., "I'm a breast man" or "I love long legs")

7. Are you in a relationship right now?

_____ Yes _____ No
(if no, skip to question 9)

8. What kind of relationship is it?

_____ Committed

_____ Casual

_____ "I don't even like her ass, I'm just biding my time."

9. *What was your last relationship like?*

_____ Committed

_____ Casual

_____ "I didn't even like her ass, I was just biding my time."

10. *What was the cause of the break-up?*

11. *How many sexual relationships do you have, and do they know about each other?*

12. *How often do you have sex? (list number of times)*

_____ Every day (You lucky sonofabitch)

_____ Every week

_____ Every month

_____ Never, I'm a virgin (You lying sonofabitch)

13. *How often do you orgasm?*

_____ Every time (You lying sonofabitch)

_____ Sometimes

_____ Never (Maybe you should see a doctor)

14. Where is the strangest place you ever did "the nasty"?

15. What's your favorite position? (This has nothing to do with the book, I'm just a nosy sonofabitch)

16. Describe your dream woman. *Please be as descriptive as you can.*

17. What was the worst date you ever had? *Please be as descriptive as you can.*

18. What was the best date you ever had? *Please be as descriptive as you can.*

You Are the Right One, Baby!

This series of questions was intended to allow the people taking the survey to choose characteristics that they most want in their mates. I wish that when you met someone new, they came with a little tag attached to their belly button that advised you of all of their features. Kind of like when you shop for a new appliance. You know—*this iron comes equipped with steam heat feature, auto on/off switch, six fabric settings, two-year warranty, and Good Housekeeping's seal of approval. This brother comes with wit, charm, his own home, a seven-inch member, desire for a long-term relationship, and your mother's seal of approval. Or you might find this in the used bin—this man has been dropped several times and some of his functions might be a little slow. The management offers no guarantee.*

The Results of My Survey

WHAT DO YOU LOOK FOR IN A MATE?

I asked people to look at the following qualities and assign a number to describe each one's importance: ranging from 2 = most important to 0 = I don't give a damn. Here are the average answers. The only things that surprised me were that I thought height was more important to women and all men preferred huge hooters. Go figure.

Quality	Women	Men
Intelligence	2	2
Education	1	1
Sense of humor	2	2
Height	1	1
Career	2	2
Morals	2	2
Community activism	1	1
Religion	1	1
Hygiene	2	2
Financial status	2	1
Penis size	2	--
Breast size	--	1
Fashion sense	1	1

You might be wondering, what does Miss Kim look for in a mate? Perfection, but if I can't get that I'll take the following:

Intelligence—This is vital to me. I want someone who is eager to learn and willing to teach. Dum-dums are no fun.

Education—Doesn't really matter that much, I mean he must have at least finished high school, but you don't have to have lots of degrees to be with me.

Sense of Humor—is ultra important. I love laughter in my

life because I create it for a living. A serious sour-puss would be wrong for me.

Height—He must have because I am tall, 5'9", and I like 'em big. And tall, that is.

Career—I have one, so should he. You can't sit at home all day watching cartoons, eating Mac and cheese. Get a job.

Morals—I don't want a pimp, but I don't want a puritan either.

Community Activism—You don't have to be a politician, but you at least have to vote.

Religion—Spirituality and awareness are far more meaningful to me than having your own reserved pew every Sabbath. A lot of people sin all week and try to be righteous on Sunday.

Hygiene—My olfactory system is so sensitive that if I don't like a person's regular natural scent I can't even be their friend, let alone lie up with them. Please bathe regularly.

Financial Status—I am more concerned about where a man is going than his already being there. I'll even point him in the right direction, but don't expect me to carry him all the way.

Penis Size—Big guns aren't necessarily better, small guns can pack quite a punch too, just know how to use the weapon you have been issued. Ready, aim, fire.

Fashion Sense—You do not have to look like the cover of *GQ* or *Ebony Man*, but at least buy well-fitting, well-made clothing, even if you have to wait for a sale, and keep your clothing laundered, please.

WHICH SKIN COLOR DO YOU PREFER?

I know that we are not supposed to focus on light skin versus dark anymore, but let's be honest, people *do* have preferences, and is there really anything wrong with that? For example, based on my past choices it is very evident that I love a darker hue. Maybe opposites attract, maybe I am trying to make up for all the Caucasian in my own personal family tree. Whatever the reason, give me an Original Man—anything in the range between coffee and midnight and I am haaaaapy!

The order of preference for women surveyed is as follows: cinnamon; caramel; a tie between mocha, dark chocolate, coffee, and vanilla with nuts (Italian); dark chocolate, butterscotch, and vanilla, licorice.

The fellas like it like this: mocha, caramel, coffee, cinnamon, dark chocolate, vanilla with or without nuts, butterscotch, licorice.

Quite a few of the respondents made comments :

"I'll take any skin as long as it's healthy"

"I like them blue-black, almost purple"

"Could be green, as long as she is a woman"

"I hate that pasty translucent vampire look, put her back in the oven"

"I prefer all the flavors from French vanilla to Midnight black"

"No pimples, please, get some Clear-a-skin, or Oxyface, something"

WHAT TYPE OF HAIR DO YOU PREFER ON YOUR MATE'S HEAD?

Men—curly, straight, braids, dreadlocks, weave, bald.

"Just as long as her hair doesn't look like Kevin Costner's in his last four movies, we are cool"

"I don't mind a weave, just tie that shit down tight. I don't want to run my fingers through and get stuck"

"I hate fuzzy braids, looks like a bird's nest"

"If she is bald, she can wear wigs, then I got them all"

"Depends on her head shape; a big onion head don't look good with an itty-bitty afro."

Women—curly, wavy, afro, bald, dreadlocks, straight.

"A regular fade, please"

"I like a tight little afro, and shape up your edges, fellas"

"Bald is hot and sexy!"

"If you are bald don't get one of those ugly rugs, just go au natural"

"I just want it clean, and combed, and no lice"

"I don't mean any disrespect, but I can't have no nappy-headed brother messing my future babies' hair up"

WHAT BODY TYPE DO YOU PREFER?
(In order of preference)

Men—regular, big mamma, long and lean, petite.

Women—regular, teddy bear, slim, muscle man, big poppa.

WHAT KIND OF VOICE DO YOU PREFER?
(I only polled women)

Most women really like a man with a deep bass voice. Although, one lady said, "Articulation is what I care about, forget the pitch, as long he has something to say, we can deal."

WHAT IS YOUR FAVORITE BODY PART?
(I asked only men)

In no particular order: butt, ass, behind, booty, long legs, traffic-stopping legs, full lips, small breasts, huge knockers, big eraser-like nipples, flat tummy, little round belly, hips, pootang, nice feet, no claws, as long as the proportion is right, I like all the parts, the eyes don't lie, cheekbones, toes, nape of neck, I'm into brains.

DESCRIBE YOUR DREAM MATE

Ladies: My dream man is: intelligent, sensitive, well-groomed, healthy, experienced, ambitious, a skillful lover, honest, faithful, gentle, a lover of animals, tall, nice, romantic, Puerto Rican, independent, open, neat, not a snorer, athletic, my husband, an all-around good guy, a great lover, Cedric Ceballos, the first James Bond, Heavy D, Denzel Washington, Antonio Banderas, Grant Hill, Mel Gibson, Brad Pitt, real, Penny Hardaway, sensual, Shaq, Greg Kinnear, disease-free, a thugish ruggish bone, is good to his mamma, cool, in great shape, Italian, 32–45 years old, not loud, very handsome, a good friend, outgoing, 6'3", not arrogant, crazy about me.

Men: My dream lady is: independent, educated, religious, sexy, a decent cook, fitness conscious, a great lover, beautiful, tall, 5'5", at least 6 feet, goal oriented, off-beat, balanced, open, Erika Alexander, Jayne Kennedy, fun, quiet, equally at home in the projects and the Serenghetti, a cross between Halle Berry and Holly Robinson, Nubian, smart, Pam Grier, sensitive, peaceful, Maya Angelou, my wife, not afraid to say no, feminine, Vesta before she lost weight, Jada Pinkett if she gained some weight, a hot Cuban chick, kind, loyal, very positive, a homebody, a party girl, a Cancer, a Capricorn, not into that bullshit astrology, secure, a slut, passionate, crazy, you.

My dream lady has: lips that can suck the paint off a '72 Chevy, a good family background, a decent job, a great sense of humor, a love of music, a green card, caramel skin, grace, looks like Vanessa Del Rio, her own life, a voice like Vanessa Williams's, athletic legs, a nice fat ass, enough time for me, money, good genes, long hair, short afro, big juicy red lips, no hump, style, classic good looks, charm, a rock-hard flat tummy, experience, warmth, no desire for kids, a lot of frilly dresses, large brown eyes, big bazooms, itty-bitty titties, inner and outer beauty, strength, a damn job, no chunks of metal sticking out of her face/mouth/bellybutton.

My dream lady can: enjoy sporting events with me, give what she gets, think big, always come to me in a crisis, remember to wash her ass, screw at the drop of a hat, love me forever, bring home the bacon and fry it up in a pan, read my mind, be honest, withstand adversity, hold her liquor, have large offspring, will stand by me, play the saxophone, at least count to ten.

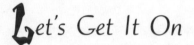et's Get It On

Supposedly what separates us humans from the animal kingdom is our ability to think. Well, my friends and associates think too damn much based on some of the imaginative places they found to "get down."

WHERE IS THE STRANGEST PLACE YOU EVER DID "THE NASTY"?

In a park after it closed, in an apartment in France with the windows wide open (*ooo la la*), on a washing machine, boyfriend's parents' backyard, Dodger Stadium parking lot, kitchen floor, kitchen sink, kitchen counter, artist's studio on a drafting table (*thank goodness, no splinters*), hood of a car at a drive-in movie, church parking lot with priest knocking on the window, bathroom on a Greyhound bus, Hellfire (an S&M club), a treehouse, on the street in front of someone's house, movie theater, airplane, lifeguard chair, the bushes in the eighth grade, a closet, a closed elementary school, a golf course (talk about a hole in one), pool table (talk about balls in the side pocket), parked cars, moving cars, during a hike to Joshua tree, on top of a dryer in a garage, on the toilet, the bathroom, lecture hall in college, in a porno theater, the Shakespeare section of the college library, on top of old Smoky all covered with snow, the storage area of an art store, in a tent with the National Guard swooping down, limo, beach, the Smithsonian Museum of African American History, swimming pool, and a bed (borrrring).

HOW OFTEN DO YOU DO IT?

The average was at least once a week for everyone. By the way, contrary to old beliefs, today's men do prefer a woman with some experience instead of a virgin. So all the ho's in the house go HO!

Hey, Why Don't We Swing from the Chandelier?

Whew! I sure know some very interesting, very imaginative, very freaky, very limber people. Hey, are ya'll wearing condoms?

WHAT IS YOUR FAVORITE POSITION?

Women—doggy style, doggy style while looking in a mirror, doggy style while hoping he remembers who he's with, straddling on top, me riding the big black horse, standing up, sixty-nine, every which way but loose, missionary, whatever feels good, me on my side with my back to him, anally, handcuffed to the bed, on my stomach with him spanking my butt, they are all good unless he weighs over 250 pounds, his face between my legs, none of your business, I'll never tell! *(That was my answer, by the way.)*

Men—doggy style, doggy style while spanking that ass, deep controlling penetrating aggressive doggy style all night, me on top ruling, her on top ruling, standing—bend over baby, I take it any way she give it to me, sixty-nine, sideways, woman sitting on my face, my own hand, on top of Kim *(I have no idea who said this)*, me lying on my back with her sitting facing the other way, missionary, come over to my house, I'll have to show you *(I have no idea who said this either)*, any position as long as I am in there, the wombat position *(what the hell is that?)*

❨ Like You, I Really Like You

The answers I received delighted me, renewed my faith in romance, and gave me some good ideas for future dates.

WHAT WAS THE BEST DATE YOU EVER HAD?

"Still waiting"

"A woman brought me flowers, took me to dinner, and she drove too. When we got home she did a striptease

for me, gave me head until I passed out and then left without expecting anything."

"You'll have to wait for my book."

"I finally got to go out with someone I'd admired for a year. We had dinner, drinks, and went dancing. We drove to Malibu to watch the ocean and made love on the beach. It was beautiful even though I had sand up my ass and it was cold."

"A riverboat cruise, seafood dinner, a carriage ride around the French quarter, and delicious beignets."

"My best date was also my worst. It was the summer of '92, I was living in Tahiti. I was walking beside a quiet blue lagoon and spotted the beautiful woman of my dreams collecting seashells. I initiated conversation, I spoke bad French, she spoke bad English, and we laughed and laughed and ate papaya as the warm blue South Pacific waters lapped at our feet. We decided to rent a small boat and sail out to watch the sunset. As we drifted, the boat hit a submerged rock and she fell in and drowned. Boy what a date!"

"An older person told me that the best sex was unexpected sex. This is so true. I ran into a friend I hadn't seen in years and went over to her house to just catch up. Next thing I know we are having teeth-gnashing, sheet-gripping, boot-knocking, bed-rocking sex. I swear we must've done it for five hours, including fore- and in between-play."

"I'll tell you what my best date would be, hook me up with Angela Bassett and Halle Berry for a ménage à trois."

"A Japanese-themed hot tub room. Two hours in the tub and on the floor."

"I was blindfolded, put on a plane, and thrown out (with a parachute). I was too thrilled to be mad."

"We flew to New York for a romantic Valentine's Day."

"I went hiking, which we Jewish girls don't usually do. I was so scared I'd fall off the mountain I couldn't be superficial on the date, and he liked that, and so did I."

"When I have it, I'll let you know."

"My senior prom. I was madly in love and he took me out for my first lobster."

"When: Valentine's Day 1989. Where: was a moonlight cruise on a private yacht. How: unforgettable sex on the deck under the stars. What: a gift of a beautiful diamond ring. Why: did we break up? Who: knows, but I kept the ring."

"I was at a party and saw this attractive man with the best-shaped lips I'd ever seen. We never really had a date because once he saw me he never left my side. I married him three years later."

"My boyfriend and I got all dressed up wearing the same colors and looked good together. I got my hair and nails done and he had a fresh haircut and got the car washed and we went out and really enjoyed each other."

"I went out with a true gentleman: opened and closed all doors, wouldn't let me touch a door handle, pulled out and pushed in all chairs, and stood when I left for and returned from the ladies' room. He was even patient while I decided what I wanted to eat. When he took me home he asked permission to kiss me goodnight. With all that good behavior I gave him the works."

"My best dates always end with hot sex."

"The best date I ever had did not even start out as a date. I knew she had a boyfriend but as luck would have it, she and I were on a fundraising committee and after the function we were left to clean up. We went to get some food, then walked around under the stars and discussed how we would change the world. A few days later she broke up with her man and moved back to New York. I still get an occasional postcard."

"That time you invited me back to your place and finally gave me some. Hey, girl, call me sometime." (Oh, how did this slip in here?)

"I fell in love with this older man and every date was heaven. He would always come to my apartment, cook for me, and then make incredible love to me. Too bad he was married."

"My man surprised me with a weekend in San Francisco. We took a hot shower and then he threw me on the bed, poured champagne all over my body, and begged me to marry him."

"It was New Year's Eve and the man I had been dating had twisted his ankle and could not go out. So I made a lovely dinner, put it into a picnic basket, got all dolled up, and went over to his place. Guess what? You don't have to use your ankle to have good sex."

"The best date I can remember was with a gorgeous physician. We had a wonderful dinner at an outdoor restaurant at South Street Seaport. Naturally, I had too much to drink but the alcohol cast a nice mellow tone on the evening. We drove in his black BMW with the top down over the Verrazano-Narrows Bridge. The evening ended romantically with a sweet kiss and roses."

"The best date I ever had was taking my fiancée out for breakfast at I.H.O.P. after getting back together with her. Finally my prayers had been answered after 129 days without her. Who knew that blueberry pancakes could win her back?"

"He came from Europe, we spent a week in a hotel room, and I smiled for a week after."

"I was going through a period of adjustment and wanted to change the types of things I was looking for in a woman. No more quick lays. I met someone and we went to the movies, had dinner, great conversation, and no physical contact, not even a kiss. Great date."

"It was only lunch. I ran into someone I hadn't seen since high school. She looked good and she felt good too when I hugged her hello. She was cute and funny and smart. All during lunch, you could cut through the sexual tension with a knife. But a man of my marital status cannot indulge in fantasies, so I never did follow up."

And what was Kim's own personal best? Well, I went out with a man who devised a way to surprise me with a single different flower with a personalized message attached to each throughout the course of the evening. We arrived at the restaurant, the maître d' handed me a rose. The meal came, the waiter gave me a lily. Dessert was accompanied by an iris. Back at the car, the valet gave me a fragrant gardenia. We drove to Mulholland Drive, cuddled, and then when he went to his trunk to get a "jacket," out came a cute Gerber daisy. When the date was over, he walked me to the door and out of nowhere came a beautiful orchid. I was really impressed because he had spent some time orchestrating this intricate plan to delight me. What a sweet man.

I Hate You, I Really Hate You

We all have been out with people who were loud and wrong, rude and wrong, stupid and wrong, and just plain **wrong**.

WHAT WAS THE WORST DATE?

"I took a woman whom I had met through a mutual friend to a concert. She tried continually and unsuccessfully to use verbal and nonverbal communication to convey how attracted she was to me. It made her seem too desperate. After several "no's" I insisted we end the evening. As I drove her home she cursed at me and told me I had missed the fuck of a lifetime."

"I was on a dinner date that was going smoothly until she suddenly pulls a knife on me. I ran and never looked back. Was there something in the salad dressing?"

"I went out with a guy and we 'happened' to run into his old girlfriend. She saw us and began to cry. He knew she would be there. For the rest of the evening he swooned over me, always sneaking to see if she was looking. He used me to make her jealous."

"Never go shopping on a first date. I left her standing in the store."

"The bitch got so drunk that she fell down and threw up all over the dance floor. Oh yeah, she was terrible in bed too. She fell asleep. Imagine that."

"Don't go on dates anymore. I'm going to live in a monastery."

"I needed my cable repaired and the guy was kind of cute. He called the next day (he got my number from the company records) and I agreed to a date. Like I said, he was cute. We went to a diner. We ate bad cheese sandwiches and our conversation was weak. He had never been to a play, didn't like to read, had no interests besides playing video games, which is okay if you are seventeen, not thirty-eight. Big zero!"

"No date is ever 'a worst.' I am just happy to get one at all."

"My date took me to see *Friday the 13th* on Friday the 13th. I guess he thought I would grab all over him from fright. I got so scared that I peed in my pants. Now that is bad luck."

"I thought it was time to introduce my new man to my old friends. We went to our favorite neighborhood pub. He started acting jealous and picked fights with them and left the bar in a huff. I stayed because I preferred the company of my friends. When I got home he was sitting outside, in the pouring rain, on the steps of my apartment building, moping, talking about 'You don't love me no more.' I dropped his ass fast."

"My then girlfriend wanted me to meet her friends. So I agreed to hang out with them at this sleazy neighborhood bar that they obviously frequent a little too much. They got too tipsy and started interrogating me like I was a criminal or something. Since I didn't want to argue, I got up and left, knowing that my girl would come to my defense and leave with me. So I waited outside her building, fuming, and then it began to drizzle. When she finally came home I told her I didn't love her anymore and I broke up with her." (Sounds like two sides of the same damn story.)

"Once we sat down at the table in the restaurant, he kept acting like he was pulling up his socks so he could look at my legs."

"I was reading aloud from Kim Coles's new book to my man when he confessed that he was the previous worst date."

"I went out with a very stupid woman that I was only attracted to sexually. We went to see a foreign film, she said she hated reading subtitles. Yes we did have sex, but it was like making love to a mannequin. Big boobs don't mean everything."

"I went out with someone who never stopped talking. Yap Yap Yap Yap Yap. All I could see was a blur of teeth and gums."

"We met, we screwed, I got crabs."

"My high school prom. His tux was too tight, he was telling everyone he was going to have sex with me, and he danced all night with my best friend doing really bad Michael Jackson 'Billie Jean' moves."

"I once went out with a very well-dressed man and complimented him on his suit. He then proceeded to lecture me that although his jacket and pants were the same color, fabric and designer, they were by no stretch of the imagination a suit. He was the epitome of dull."

"Do you have any money?" "No, do you?"

"A man invited me to a home-cooked meal. His house was so dirty, I couldn't eat anything."

"I dated a comedian who I thought was so funny. When we hung out he turned out to be a dark, brooding, intense man. That only works for James Dean or Laurence Fishburne."

"Blind date, don't do it. I got my friend to set me up with my favorite deejay at the radio station. Well, they should change the letters to WYUK. He had jagged front teeth, huge water pimples, and body odor. But his voice was like velvet."

"We went to an expensive restaurant and the waiter mistakenly only wrote down one order. When my date's food arrived and mine didn't, my date suggested that it would be fun if we shared. As I got up to leave, he confessed that on the way to the restroom he told the waiter to cancel my order because he didn't have enough money for two entrees."

"I went out with this girl to the movies and I thought we had a good time, but she never returned my calls."

"Bowling, so dull."

"Thankfully, my mind won't let me remember."

"He was a thug, smoked a joint, didn't offer me any, and had the nerve to want sex."

"My date was 'tore up from the floor up.'"

"My date spent the whole time looking at his reflection in a spoon."

"I opened the door and there he was, carrying a bag of groceries, and said, 'Hell, girl, anybody can bring you flowers. I brought you something you can use.' Oh yeah, I can use a forty-ounce bottle of Old English, some Spam, and generic saltines."

"He was late, he was ugly, and he talked on his cellular phone at the table."

"She was too thin, didn't touch her food, and excused herself to the bathroom several times. She was either a drug addict or bulimic."

"Everything was beautiful until I turned her over. Her ass was stinking!"

"Went on the date and he started to go into convulsions. I'm thinking heart attack, turns out it was an asthma attack and he had left his medication at home. Luckily someone had some Primatine Mist or something."

"Never had a worst date. The minute I sense things aren't going well, I treat it like a hotel fire: Stay low to the ground, and get the hell out!"

And as for me, well, I am lucky. I have three worst dates:

1. This guy I met in college who had raw onions on his burger. We sat in his car talking and I swore I could see a blue funk coming from his mouth. No kiss goodnight. I would've fainted.

2. I went out to dinner with a man who not only chewed with his mouth open, he never wiped his mouth afterward. He had eaten fried chicken, and he had greasy, shiny lips. Kind of like an oil slick. No kiss goodnight. I would have fallen off.

3. I met a handsome older man at a party. We sat and talked. I agreed to a date because he was charming and intelligent. When he came to pick me up, I noticed for the first time that he had a really pronounced limp. Like one leg was at least twelve inches shorter than the other. I felt really bad for no longer being attracted to him so I decided to rise above this mild handicap. And I am proud to say I did. Kiss goodnight—yes. And then I discovered his real handicap: He had a limp credit rating and was lame in the wallet. And I knew he would have eventually tried to use my account as a crutch. No more kisses.

ABOUT THE AUTHOR

Kim Coles does it all. She is a comedian, actress, play-wright, producer, and now author. While working in the fashion business in New York during the day, she started doing stand-up comedy in clubs at night. Then Holly-wood came a-calling and she began working as an open-ing act for Luther Vandross and Sinbad, doing national Burger King commercials, and was an original cast mem-ber on "In Living Color."

Kim plays the lovable Synclaire James on Fox's hit sitcom series "Living Single." As if all this wasn't enough, this workaholic decided to try her hand at theater, so she wrote and produced *Homework*, her own semi-autobiographical one-woman show. *Homework* received critical acclaim in Los Angeles and the show is on its way to New York for more of the same. Kim, a native of the world's best borough, Brooklyn, now resides in the not-so-bad city of Los Angeles.